IMAGES
of America

US ROUTE 1
BALTIMORE TO
WASHINGTON, DC

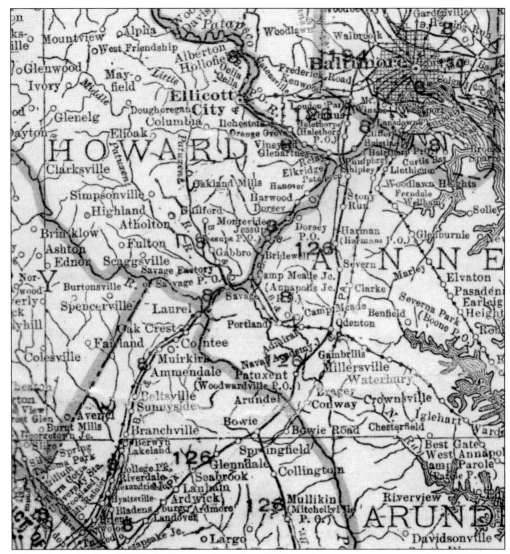

Taken from the *Rand McNally Commercial Atlas* of 1924, this map shows the corridor of US Route 1 and the Baltimore & Ohio Railroad between Washington, DC, and Baltimore. Communities along the route include Bladensburg, Hyattsville, College Park, and Laurel in Prince George's County; Annapolis Junction and Elkridge in Howard County; and Relay and Halethorpe in Baltimore County. (National Archives and Records Administration.)

ON THE COVER: Cars and buses travel along US Route 1 just outside of Savage, Maryland, in this 1939 photograph from the National Archives and Records Administration Bureau of Public Roads Collection. Littered with billboards, hotels, gas stations, and telephone poles, this roadside scene was common in the landscape between Baltimore and Washington. (National Archives and Records Administration.)

IMAGES
of America

US ROUTE 1
BALTIMORE TO
WASHINGTON, DC

Aaron Marcavitch

ARCADIA
PUBLISHING

Published by Arcadia Publishing
Charleston, South Carolina

Printed in the United States of America

Library of Congress Control Number: 2017941244

For all general information, please contact Arcadia Publishing:
Telephone 843-853-2070
Fax 843-853-0044
E-mail sales@arcadiapublishing.com
For customer service and orders:
Toll-Free 1-888-313-2665

Visit us on the Internet at www.arcadiapublishing.com

Dedicated to Andrea, Beatrice, and Graham
for their support of my love of roadside architecture.

To my parents for nurturing a love of history.

CONTENTS

ACKNOWLEDGMENTS

When the Anacostia Trails Heritage Area was certified in 2001, there was a focus on the importance of transportation and communication history within the corridor as an interpretive element. However, that focus was left to others to detail. I sincerely hope this volume will highlight the central story of the US Route 1 corridor as a major force in transportation and communications history within Maryland and the United States.

I would most like to thank Prince George's County Historical Society historian Susan Pearl for her previous documentation of US Route 1, her help and guidance, and her editing during this project. The introduction was written in part based on her previous work. Thanks also to the Howard County Historical Society, Baltimore Public Library System, College Park Aviation Museum, Elkridge Historical Society, Maryland–National Capital Park and Planning Commission Natural and Historic Resources Division, New York Public Library, Southern Methodist University, Library of Congress, National Archives and Records Administration, DC Public Library Special Collections, National Capital Trolley Museum, and Baltimore & Ohio Railroad Museum for their time, collections, and resources. Thanks to the board of Anacostia Trails Heritage Area Inc., and the staff of Patapsco Heritage Greenway for their support during this project.

Finally, I would like to thank my parents for instilling a love of history of all types, my wife for supporting my wild research projects, and my children for their enthusiasm for the things I love.

INTRODUCTION

Stretching from the Baltimore city line to the Washington, DC, boundary are a variety of residential communities and commercial crossroads clustered along both sides of multiple historically important arteries of transportation—US Route 1, the Baltimore & Ohio Railroad's Washington Branch, the Baltimore-Washington Parkway, and US Interstate 95. Traveling north to south, this area includes the communities of Halethorpe, Relay, Elkridge, Dorsey, Annapolis Junction, Jessup, Savage, Laurel, Beltsville, College Park, Berwyn Heights, Greenbelt, University Park, Riverdale Park, Hyattsville, North Brentwood, Brentwood, Mount Rainier, and on the original alignment of Route 1, Edmonston, Bladensburg, Cottage City, and Colmar Manor. "America's Main Street" has seen milestones in both the physical and figurative sense, marking the major moments in American history. Yet this corridor has seen so much change in nearly three centuries that visitors and residents are often unable to see the history beneath their feet. This is the landscape—a landscape that geographer Pierce F. Lewis might have meant when he wrote "our human landscape is our unwitting autobiography"—that will be explored herein.

EARLY TRANSPORTATION ROUTE
Prior to European settlers arriving in the region, the area covered by this volume was home to the Nacotchtank and Pawtuxunt tribes. They used paths and rivers for transportation. However, much of this history is unwritten or apocryphal. Therefore, this introduction intentionally starts after European arrival and about the time the first communities were being established.

The area through which US Route 1 now runs was still rural and agricultural in character in the early 18th century. The establishment of Elkridge Landing and Bladensburg would change that landscape. Elkridge Landing was established in 1734 by an act of the Maryland General Assembly for a 30-acre site on the banks of the Patapsco River with 40 lots. Bladensburg was established at Garrison's Landing on the Eastern Branch of the Potomac in 1742 by the General Assembly, with commissioners appointed to purchase 60 acres and lay out a town of 60 one-acre lots.

Both Elkridge Landing and Bladensburg initially thrived, becoming important port towns with wharves, taverns, and stores. In 1747, five years after Bladensburg's establishment, the General Assembly passed "An Act to Amend the Staple of Tobacco" and established tobacco ports by providing for a wharf, scales, warehouse, and inspector at each port of entry. Bladensburg and Elkridge Landing became major ports collecting tobacco from the surrounding areas. However, both communities would suffer from their success. At Elkridge Landing, the riverbed began filling with sand ballast from the ships that used the port, closing it to ships by the mid-1700s. Bladensburg also suffered from silting, in its case caused by erosion from tobacco farms upstream of the Eastern Branch, rendering the former deep-water port unnavigable by 1835, just as the railroad arrived and bypassed the center of town.

By the middle of the 18th century, as the ports were booming, a roadway connecting Baltimore to Georgetown via Elkridge Landing and Bladensburg came into use. As early as 1741, a road had connected Baltimore with Elkridge Landing. This road is clearly shown on a map of Maryland produced in 1794; the roadway crossed the Patapsco River at Elkridge Landing, crossed the Patuxent River at a point near the Snowden Iron Furnace, and ran in a southwesterly direction through Bladensburg and the capital city to Georgetown. By the 1790s, taverns had been established along its course, some frequented by George Washington; a mail route was started; and consideration was being given to making the route a toll road.

In 1812, the State of Maryland chartered a company that sought to build a turnpike between Washington and Baltimore, using much of the existing right-of-way. The road was set out to be

60 feet wide, beginning at the corner of Pratt and Eutaw Streets at the western Baltimore city limits, crossing the Patapsco River at Elkridge Landing via Norwood's Ferry, passing Snowden's Iron Works, the tavern at Vansville, White House Tavern two miles south, and Ross's Tavern three miles farther south, and continuing through Bladensburg and then into the District of Columbia. Tolls were collected every 10 miles and were levied per the number of vehicles and animals. Along the right-of-way were milestones, only one of which has survived. The stone that stood on the grounds of the White House Tavern in Beltsville reads "25 M[iles] to B[altimore]."

These taverns represented an important part of communications history. Elkridge Landing and Bladensburg were both colonial mail stops on the route established in 1717 under the British. During the revolutionary period, a new mail route system was established, this time with Bladensburg as the only stop between Baltimore and Washington. Mail coaches, changing horses and loading passengers at taverns, brought news of the world via newspapers, mail, and gossip.

The turnpike operated until 1865, when the charter was revoked and the counties were given control of the road. Many reasons were given for the revocation, but the biggest reason was the arrival of the railroad 30 years earlier. The Baltimore & Ohio Railroad began operations in 1835, and soon after that, traffic on the turnpike began to decrease, replaced by the convenience of the new railroad. In defense against their new competitor, the turnpike directors began to decrease turnpike tolls. Maintenance of the road consequently deteriorated, and by the period of the Civil War, the turnpike was in serious trouble.

THE RAILROAD CONQUERS
The Baltimore & Ohio Railroad's Washington Branch was the first rail link between the nation's capital and the rest of the growing country. Within months of opening, the Washington Branch was the most heavily trafficked rail line in the United States. By 1838, US mail was carried on the branch, replacing the mail coach. The branch begins at Relay, so named for the point at which horses had been swapped out when they pulled the railcars. Diverging from the "old main line," which ran to Ellicott City, the branch starts atop the Thomas Viaduct, a marvel of engineering crossing the Patapsco River. With eight great stone arches, the viaduct was the longest bridge in the United States and second largest in the world at the time of its completion in 1835. The route then parallels the US Route 1 corridor through Elkridge and Savage, crossing the Patuxent River at Laurel Factory and running south toward Bladensburg and into the District of Columbia.

The construction of the railroad changed the patterns of travel, commerce, and daily life for residents of the area. Men began to conduct business at some distance from their residence; many businessmen purchased discount tickets for regular local travel to ride from their rural homes into either Washington or Baltimore. Two passenger trains ran round-trip each day, carrying an average of 200 passengers a day; the trip between the two cities took two hours. Stations were established at several locations along the railroad line, and small communities began to develop there: towns like Jessup, Dorsey, Savage, Beltsville, Branchville, Riverdale Park, and Hyattsville. These communities were brought into existence by the construction of the railroad.

Other railroads that served the region included the Annapolis & Elk Ridge, chartered in 1837 to serve Annapolis from a point near Savage, and the Baltimore & Potomac Railroad, established in 1872. The Baltimore & Potomac was later controlled by the Pennsylvania Railroad and crossed the Baltimore & Ohio line near Halethorpe before crossing the Annapolis & Elk Ridge at Odenton and entering Prince George's County at Bowie. Both lines would prove important to the region.

Another communications development that changed the landscape was the electromagnetic telegraph. In 1844, the first telegraph line was constructed within the Baltimore & Ohio Railroad right-of-way by inventors Samuel F.B. Morse, who developed the telegraph, and Ezra Cornell, who oversaw the pole installation. One of the first tests of the line was made near Riversdale, where Morse had established a test site. History remembers Morse's famous "What hath God wrought" message sent between Baltimore and Washington; much of the initial work on the system was performed in this US Route 1 corridor.

The Civil War brought a new impact to the region. Troops were stationed at points along the Baltimore & Ohio Railroad: Relay, Annapolis Junction, and in Bladensburg at Fort Lincoln and Camp Casey. Multiple Union units were stationed in Laurel, noting that engineers would not run a train without Laurel under guard. In 1864, the small community of Beltsville was the site of a Confederate detachment of troops that destroyed the rail line and burned railcars. This cavalry was led by Bradley Johnson, who served under Jubal Early during the attack on Washington, DC.

TRAINS, TROLLEYS, AND PLANES ALONG ROUTE 1

After the Civil War and during the later decades of the 19th century, residential suburbs began to develop along the lines of the railroad and the old turnpike. Hyattsville, near Bladensburg's station on the main line, was established in 1885. A year after Hyattsville's founding, 475 acres of the Riversdale plantation, including the mansion, were sold to a New York real estate syndicate that began development of the suburb of Riverdale Park. Communities such as College Park, Brentwood, and Mount Rainier followed. The community of North Brentwood was part of an 1891 plat by Capt. Wallace Bartlett. The community provided a place for black farmers and laborers to live, some of whom were associated with Bartlett by their service in the US Colored Troops in the Civil War. This was the first majority black community to be incorporated in Prince George's County.

Streetcars began rolling into the region in the 1890s. Companies were chartered for the construction of streetcar lines between Washington and Baltimore. In 1897, trolley service began from the district line at Mount Rainier into the District of Columbia. In the next few years, this trolley line was extended by the City & Suburban Railway Company in a northeasterly direction through the developing suburbs. It followed the line of an extended Rhode Island Avenue, reaching Brentwood, North Brentwood, Hyattsville, and Riverdale Park. After 1901, the northern extension of the trolley line was undertaken by the Washington, Berwyn & Laurel Railroad Company, and in 1902, service was completed through College Park all the way to Laurel. Another line was started in 1908 running from Washington, DC, to Bladensburg. The Washington, Spa Spring & Gretta eventually went as far as Berwyn Heights, bringing new residents to the small enclave between College Park and what would later be the community of Greenbelt. The advent of the streetcar line spurred further development in these northerly subdivisions.

Running out of Baltimore, the Washington, Baltimore & Annapolis Electric Railway would parallel the region to the east, running all the way into Washington via a route near Bowie. While this route was much farther east, the line also had a "south shore" route acquired from the Annapolis & Elkridge Railroad that ran through Camp Meade.

While trains and trolleys ruled the land, there were changes in the air. In 1903, the Wright brothers had their first successful flight. The US Army recognized the importance of this technology and requested that the Wrights develop a flying school. Established first in Virginia, the school moved to a location that was accessible via train, trolley, and road: College Park. Wilbur Wright opened the school in 1909. The school remained active until 1912, when it moved to Texas. However, the airfield still operates and has seen the span of flight history, with early tests of helicopters, the first female pilot, early radio navigation, and the first tests of machine guns on planes. The airmail service was also started in College Park in 1918. Nearby were several other airports, including the Engineering and Research Corporation (ERCO) company field. The history of flight did not start with airplanes in the corridor, an honor bestowed on the early balloon tests in Bladensburg in the 1790s. Nor did it end with the airport, as NASA Goddard Space Flight Center continues the legacy of flight.

The period of World War I was a time of massive troop movements, but it was also a time when the change from rail and horse to automobile and plane was not complete. Camp Meade, today known as Fort Meade, was established in the corridor along the rail lines. Troops arrived daily for training by train, while horses left for the front lines via those same trains. Automobiles mingled with horses, while trains saw airplanes fly overhead.

THE CHANGING FACE OF ROUTE 1

Changes were still to come to the ancient road that, in the 20th century, would become US Route 1. In the later parts of the 19th century, "Good Roads" advocates called for improving major routes in the country. Many of these advocates were part of the new bicycle movement that swept across the United States. Automobile development increased locally, including unique car builders such as the Carter Motor Company in modern Edmonston.

Maryland established a roads commission, responsible for working with counties to improve and maintain routes, including the historic turnpike route. New systems for paving roads were developed. During this time, there was pressure to name major routes, such as the Lincoln Highway. The Baltimore-and-Washington route was considered part of the Atlantic Highway. That name was short lived, as agreements among states led to a numbering system, with this route designated State Highway Number 1.

New suburban pressure came during the 1930s. One major project was located off Route 1 near Berwyn and was led by the Resettlement Administration under the New Deal. Greenbelt, a planned community, was constructed near the government-owned Beltsville Agricultural Research Farm fields near Route 1. This massive project developed new housing for those in slum conditions surrounded by a "belt of green." Housing developments around the region grew and expanded. Suburbs grew father away from the city centers.

During World War II, US Route 1 and the railroads continued to serve the country. Heavy trucks rolled up and down the road, often leading to damage that was hard to manage. Later, the returning troops, and the resulting baby boom, shaped much of the landscape of the corridor.

FROM ROADS TO ROCKETS TO TODAY

As suburbs grew and private automobiles increased, pressure on US Route 1 mounted. In the 1940s, the road was seeing a crush of vehicles and associated growth. Roadside developments such as gas stations, cabins and motels, and diners of various types encroached on Route 1, pushing signs closer and closer to the driver. To move away from this crush of ugly development, government officials developed and began construction on the Baltimore-Washington Parkway in the early 1950s. This four-lane concrete highway cut through the region and connected communities, allowing for faster travel in and out of the cities without the roadside sprawl. As this new highway came into existence, trolleys and passenger trains were fading. Trolleys stopped running in the 1960s. Passenger train service was discontinued by the 1970s. Development of the Capital Beltway, the Baltimore Beltway, and Interstate 95, built to improve upon the parkway, would be made in the 1960s to decrease travel time even further, spurring more development.

Approaching the end of the 20th century, the Washington Metropolitan Area Transit Authority began construction of the Metro system with stations in Hyattsville, College Park, and Greenbelt. The Maryland Area Regional Commuter train utilizes routes on the Camden (the former Baltimore & Ohio route) and Penn (former Pennsylvania) lines to bring back the passenger train for commuters through the communities in the US Route 1 region.

Nearly three centuries ago, the US Route 1 corridor was a rural, agricultural area traversed by a north-south pathway; now the route is a heavily traveled highway through residential, commercial, and industrial areas with parallel highways and superhighways. Multiple transportation methods, now including bike trails in and out of the cities, have come together to create a complex tapestry of systems. However, beneath this transportation network is a long history of innovation in transportation and communications that has shaped America and the landscape of these communities.

—Susan Pearl and Aaron Marcavitch

One

EARLY TRANSPORTATION ROUTE

1600–1835

Early life in the tidewater landscape of Maryland was built on tobacco. In this 1700s-era print, enslaved Africans roll a hogshead of tobacco along a "rolling road" toward a tobacco ship. This scene would have been common in Elkridge Landing and Bladensburg. This coming together of road and water was a defining feature of early life in this road corridor. (Maryland Highways Administration.)

RIVER - BLADENSBURG, MD. - A/S

Prior to the arrival of European settlers to the region, native tribes inhabited the area that now includes Route 1. The Nacotchtank tribe was part of the larger Algonquin tribe that inhabited much of the eastern United States. These Nacotchtank, a name that was corrupted by English settlers to the word "Anacostia," lived by trading, fishing, and hunting in what would become the Washington, DC, region. Capt. John Smith, an early explorer of the Potomac River, first visited in 1608. He recorded massive numbers of fish, such as shad, leaping from the water. This photograph from 1909 shows children fishing in the quiet and still Anacostia River. Having silted from tobacco farming upstream, the river had lost the deep-water port almost 100 years earlier. Unfortunately, today's residents have been advised against eating fish from the Anacostia River due to pollution. Groups such as the Anacostia Watershed Society have been working hard to revitalize and clean up the Anacostia River. (DC Public Library, Wilbur Ross Postcard Collection.)

Captain Smith wrote during exploration up the Patuxent River that "Thus having sought all the inlets and rivers worth noting, we returned to discover the river of Pawtuxunt; these people we found . . . more civil than any." This 1909 photograph shows a common landscape at the fall line, the point where rocky piedmont turns to the soft soil of the coastal plains. (DC Public Library, Wilbur Ross Postcard Collection.)

Once wider and deeper than it is today, the Patapsco River runs southward, creating the Howard County boundary. The Patapsco served the port at Elkridge Landing before meeting the Chesapeake Bay below Baltimore. In the early 1600s, the river was broad and gentle east of the fall line, as shown in this 1886 photograph of the river under the Thomas Viaduct. (Howard County Historical Society.)

Travelers from around the world came to trade in Bladensburg and Elkridge Landing. The modern painting above shows a mail coach in Bladensburg at the Market Master building, still extant, where residents received and shared information. Both Bladensburg and Elkridge Landing served as mail stops as early as 1741. In the background is a tobacco ship in the deep-water port of Bladensburg. This port, like the port at Elkridge Landing, was where tobacco was weighed, packaged, and loaded before being shipped to Europe. By 1835, the port at Bladensburg was abandoned due to silting. In Elkridge Landing (pictured below), the oldest settlement in Howard County, the river was 14 feet deep, enough for large ships receiving tobacco from surrounding plantations. Just as at Bladensburg, the port at Elkridge Landing was abandoned by the mid-1800s due to silting. (Above, Maryland Highways Administration; below, Elkridge Heritage Society.)

These 1700s paintings show life in the early American colonies. The region was dominated by water access rather than roads or, later, rails. Roads at this period were functional but not well marked or maintained for long-distance travel. These roads would be used to bring tobacco and materials in from the countryside to be shipped to ports on major waterways. The image above shows the Anacostia as a wide and flat river. Bladensburg would have been located upstream, where the river narrows. In Baltimore (below), Whetstone Point is where modern Fort McHenry is located and represents the point where the Patapsco River, arriving from Elkridge Landing, meets the Inner Harbor before heading to the Chesapeake Bay. (Both, Library of Congress.)

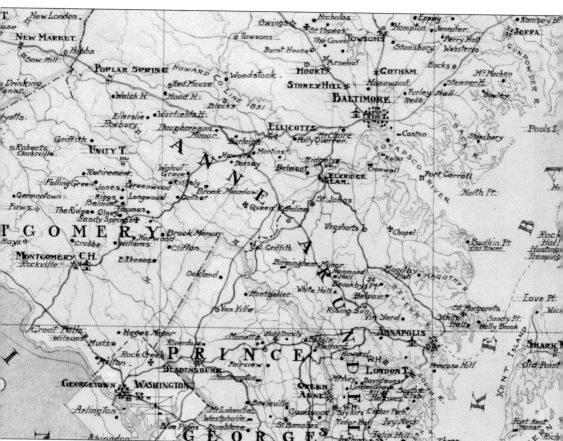

This 1933 map utilizes historic information and maps from the era to reconstruct the road landscape of 1794. Notable points, from south to north, include Bladensburg (shown as a small community at the point where several roads converge), Riversdale (listed as Riverdale here), Van Ville (or Vansville near modern Beltsville), Montpelier (near modern Laurel), Col. William Griffith's home near modern Savage, St. John's Chapel south of Elkridge Landing, and Elkridge Landing. The straighter line from Vansville to Elkridge Landing is the route of modern Route 1, while the wiggling line is the more historic overland route. Notice that the road that would become Route 1 branches and connects at Mount Claire rather than running straight into Baltimore as it does today. In 1794, roads were predominantly organized toward the Chesapeake Bay, since Washington, DC, had only been established in 1790. The only other road that ran north from Washington was the road through Montgomery County, now a portion of US Route 29. (Library of Congress.)

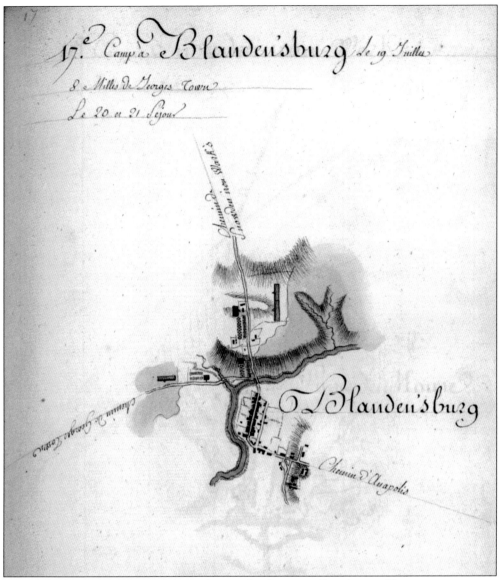

One of the first major tests of the corridor was the American Revolution. Clear, easy movement from the north to the south was vital to the success of the troops. The road between Baltimore and Georgetown was an important route, but it was not well maintained south of Elkridge or much farther north than Bladensburg. Maps developed by troops under the command of Jean Baptiste Donatien de Vimeur, comte de Rochambeau, document the camps of the troops and wagon trains as they marched north between July and December 1782. This first map shows the campsite just outside of Bladensburg, written as "Blandensburg," near where modern Hyattsville's Charles Armentrout Road is now located. The map notes the camp was eight miles from Georges Town (Georgetown) and was occupied from July 19 to 21, 1782. To the left is Georges Town via Bunker Hill Road, to the right is the road to Annapolis, while to the north is the road to Snowden Iron Works. (Library of Congress.)

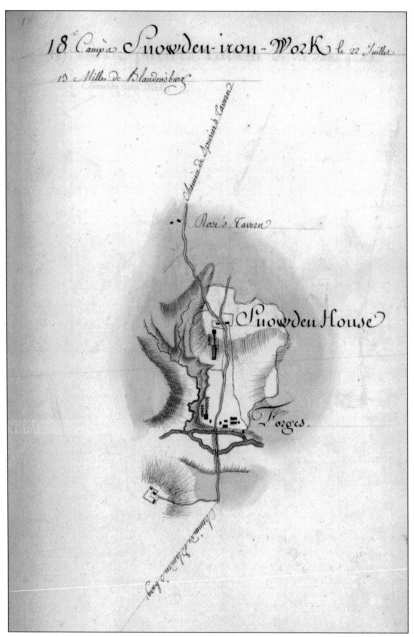

This second map shows Snowden Iron Works, located across the Patuxent River from Montpelier Mansion, 13 miles from Bladensburg via the road to the south. The road to Spurier's Tavern leads north just past Rose's Tavern. Note the word "Forges" at the river next to the cannon placement. These forges were of the Patuxent Iron Works, founded in 1705 by Richard Snowden. Charles Carroll noted in 1753 that this was the only iron works near navigable waters in Maryland. The Snowdens owned over 20,000 acres of land, including Snow Hill, Oaklands, Snowden Hall, and Montpelier in Prince George's County. The Snowden Hall on this map may be confused with Birmingham Manor, destroyed by fire in 1891. Montpelier and Snow Hill are preserved and in public use today. The location of Rochambeau's camp here would have been a restocking point for the artillery before moving north. (Library of Congress.)

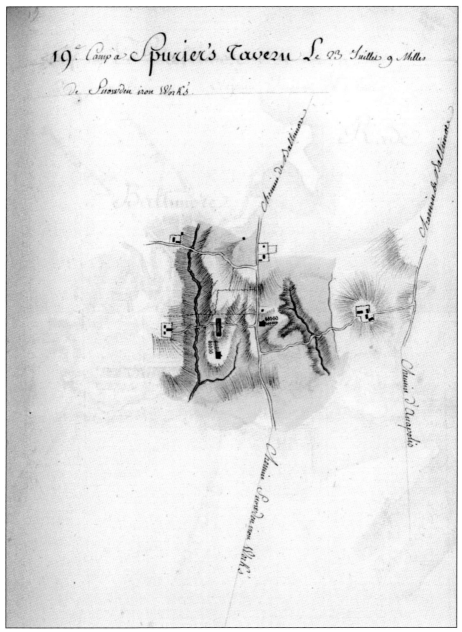

19ᵉ Camp a **Spurrier's Tavern** Le 23 Juillet 9 Milles
De Snowden iron Works

Continuing north, Rochambeau's men arrived at Spurrier's Tavern, in what is now known as Waterloo or Jessup. Built on nearly 200 acres of land owned by Thomas Spurrier, the tavern was at a major crossing point on the road to Baltimore (modern Route 1 and Maryland Route 175). During the Revolutionary War, this tavern was a major resupply point. George Washington wrote of the tavern, "dined and lodged at Spurrier's where my sick horse died." Interestingly, because the route has shifted over the years, this drawing may not be showing Route 1 in the expected manner. The side roads may be showing branches that would become Route 1, while the main branch in the middle is closer to modern Route 175. However, both northbound routes indicate they are routes to Baltimore, while the southward routes head toward Bladensburg or Annapolis. This connection point was a vital hub in the transportation network of the time. (Library of Congress.)

In the years before and following the Revolutionary War, Bladensburg was a vital part of the north-south route. The George Washington House (above) is one of the oldest buildings in Bladensburg, constructed in the 1750s. However, the pictured structure was never a tavern. The tavern where George Washington once stayed has been discovered to be located next door in a space that is now a parking lot. This structure, a store, was restored in the 1970s during the Bicentennial of the Declaration of Independence and is now the office and headquarters of the Anacostia Watershed Society. The Ross House (below) was a particularly fine brick townhouse built in 1746; it served as a field hospital during the War of 1812. Located on Annapolis Road, the Ross House was dismantled in 1957 and moved to Baltimore County for reconstruction and restoration. (Above, Prince George's County Historical Society; below, Library of Congress.)

Montpelier Mansion was one of several homes owned by the Snowden family. Constructed between 1781 and 1785, the house was built by Thomas Snowden on over 9,000 acres of land. It stayed in the Snowden family until 1890. Martha Washington stayed here on her way to the first presidential inauguration in 1789. (Library of Congress.)

The oldest house in modern Howard County, Troy, is on a hill above the Baltimore-to-Washington road. Built in 1808, the house was modified several times until 1958, when the State of Maryland bought the property for the construction of Interstate 95. The house stood in neglect for nearly 30 years before Howard County restored it as part of a much larger park environment. (Elkridge Heritage Society.)

On June 17, 1784, the owner of the George Washington House and the tavern next door performed a transportation milestone that is little remembered today. Peter Carnes, the innkeeper and a local lawyer, after reading about the Montgolfier brothers' experiments in France, went out into the fields around Bladensburg and launched the first tethered, unmanned hot air balloon in the United States. Carnes had intended to launch the balloon as a manned flight, but in the process of setting up the balloon, winds scooped up the basket, crashing it into a nearby fence. Carnes chose to leave the basket unmanned and launch anyway. He would move on to the first tethered, manned launch in the United States a week later in Baltimore with a 13-year-old boy in the basket. This launch marked the birth of aviation, right along the Baltimore-to-Washington road. (Library of Congress.)

Growing transportation between Washington and Baltimore created new pressure to maintain and keep the road in passable condition. A turnpike company was founded in 1812 and was responsible for maintaining a right-of-way of 60 feet and collecting tolls every 10 miles. Only one marker from the route remains, in Beltsville near IKEA. The marker reads "25 M[iles] to B[altimore]." (Prince George's County Historical Society.)

Crossing Dueling Creek, the bridge that carried the Washington-to-Baltimore Turnpike hid a flat area lined with trees, known as the Bladensburg Dueling Grounds. The grounds became an informal location for dueling. The practice was outlawed in Washington, DC, so duelists traveled to Bladensburg. One of the most famous of the approximately 50 duels was the Stephen Decatur–James Barron duel on March 22, 1820, in which Decatur was killed. (Library of Congress.)

THE DUEL.

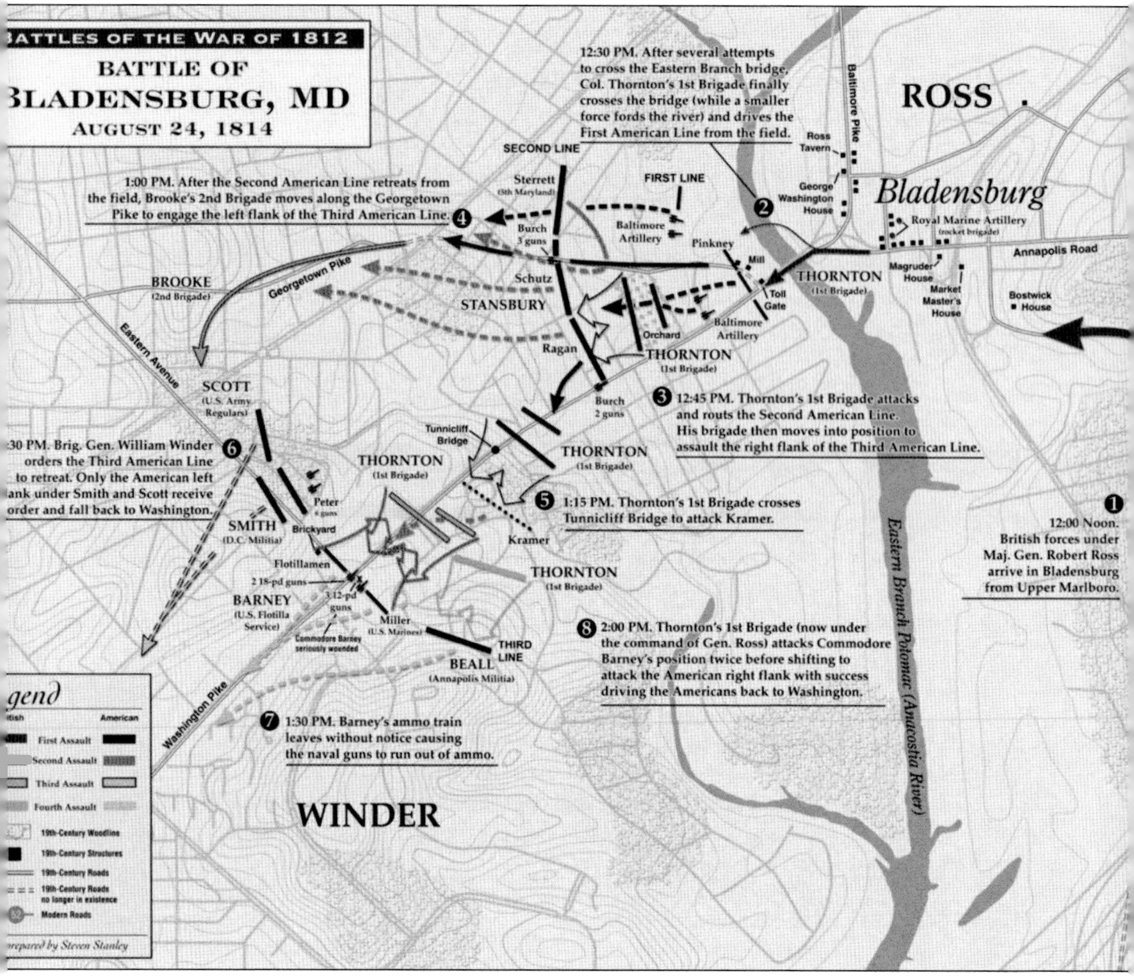
BATTLES OF THE WAR OF 1812
BATTLE OF BLADENSBURG, MD
AUGUST 24, 1814
12:30 PM. After several attempts to cross the Eastern Branch bridge, Col. Thornton's 1st Brigade finally crosses the bridge (while a smaller force fords the river) and drives the First American Line from the field.
ROSS
Baltimore Pike
Ross Tavern
George Washington House
Bladensburg
Royal Marine Artillery (rocket brigade)
Annapolis Road
Magruder House
Market Master's House
Bostwick House
SECOND LINE
FIRST LINE
1:00 PM. After the Second American Line retreats from the field, Brooke's 2nd Brigade moves along the Georgetown Pike to engage the left flank of the Third American Line.
Sterrett (5th Maryland)
Burch 3 guns
Baltimore Artillery
Pinkney
Mill
Toll Gate
THORNTON (1st Brigade)
BROOKE (2nd Brigade)
Georgetown Pike
Schutz
STANSBURY
Baltimore Artillery
Orchard
Ragan
THORNTON (1st Brigade)
Eastern Avenue
SCOTT (U.S. Army Regulars)
Burch 2 guns
12:45 PM. Thornton's 1st Brigade attacks and routs the Second American Line. His brigade then moves into position to assault the right flank of the Third American Line.
1:30 PM. Brig. Gen. William Winder orders the Third American Line to retreat. Only the American left flank under Smith and Scott receive order and fall back to Washington.
Tunnicliff Bridge
THORNTON (1st Brigade)
THORNTON (1st Brigade)
Peter 6 guns
SMITH (D.C. Militia)
Brickyard
1:15 PM. Thornton's 1st Brigade crosses Tunnicliff Bridge to attack Kramer.
Kramer
12:00 Noon. British forces under Maj. Gen. Robert Ross arrive in Bladensburg from Upper Marlboro.
Flotillamen
2 18-pd guns
3 12-pd guns
BARNEY (U.S. Flotilla Service)
Commodore Barney seriously wounded
Miller (U.S. Marines)
THORNTON (1st Brigade)
2:00 PM. Thornton's 1st Brigade (now under the command of Gen. Ross) attacks Commodore Barney's position twice before shifting to attack the American right flank with success driving the Americans back to Washington.
THIRD LINE
BEALL (Annapolis Militia)
Eastern Branch Potomac (Anacostia River)
Washington Pike
1:30 PM. Barney's ammo train leaves without notice causing the naval guns to run out of ammo.
WINDER
Legend
British
American
First Assault
Second Assault
Third Assault
Fourth Assault
19th-Century Woodline
19th-Century Structures
19th-Century Roads
19th-Century Roads no longer in existence
Modern Roads
Prepared by Steven Stanley

In 1814, the War of 1812 arrived in Maryland. Less known than the American Revolution just 40 years earlier or the Civil War just 50 years ahead, the War of 1812 was the first major test of American military might. Battles were fought on the oceans and in the Great Lakes, but the Mid-Atlantic was largely spared. However, in the late summer of 1814, British troops landed in southern Prince George's County and traveled overland toward Bladensburg, arriving around noon on August 23. The British chose Bladensburg because it allowed them to cross the river into Washington, DC, relatively easily. On the field that day leading American troops were President Madison, Secretary of State James Monroe, and Francis Scott Key. The latter would go on to Baltimore a few weeks later and write "The Star-Spangled Banner." Facing off against an ill-led, untrained, untested, and under-equipped American militia, the British forced the Americans off the field before marching on toward Dueling Grounds, where they met Commodore Joshua Barney's flotilla men. (Maryland–National Capital Park and Planning Commission.)

Born in 1759 near Savage, Maryland, Commodore Joshua Barney grew up along the upper Patuxent River. At 17, he joined the Continental Navy as a master's mate on the *Hornet*. He would be promoted to lieutenant on board the *Wasp* and showed his early prowess as a soldier and tactician. After serving in the Revolutionary War, he traveled to France and served as a captain in the French navy. He returned to the US Navy as a captain and led the Chesapeake Bay Flotilla, a small fleet of gunboats that could easily retreat to shallow water after attacking. In July 1814, his flotilla was chased up the Patuxent River, where Barney called for the ships to be scuttled to avoid British capture. His flotilla men were then stationed in Washington, DC, before abandoning their posts for the Battle of Bladensburg. (Library of Congress.)

The British forces chose Bladensburg because the Anacostia River was easy to ford this far inland. They arrived and set up their installations of rockets aimed across the new bridge built for the turnpike. From the south, Joshua Barney moved his men up the Bladensburg Road, arriving just as the British were marching toward them, having overrun the other American forces. Barney ordered cannons aimed down the turnpike, locating the artillery at the top of the hill near modern Eastern Avenue. His cannons repulsed the British multiple times, and the troops held back the British for an hour, giving time to remove documents such as the Constitution and Declaration of Independence from Washington and providing the British with their first real fight. Barney ordered retreat as the British began to overwhelm the small force, but his troops would not yield. He was eventually shot through the leg, whereupon he ordered retreat again. British officers granted him a full pardon after he surrendered because of his men's bravery and resolve, as shown in this painting. (Maryland Highways Administration.)

Two

THE RAILROAD CONQUERS

1835–1890

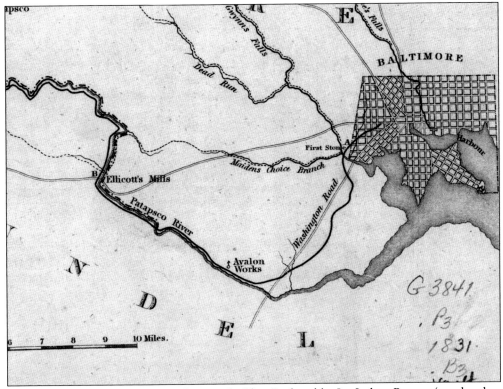

In this 1831 survey of the new Baltimore & Ohio Railroad by Lt. Joshua Barney (unrelated to the Joshua Barney wounded at Bladensburg), the route is shown passing Avalon Works near the Washington Road, headed for Ellicott's Mills. The distance from "A" to "B" was the first major railroad in Maryland. In a few years, the Washington Branch would parallel and supersede the Washington Road. (Library of Congress.)

Peter Cooper's *Tom Thumb* was the first American-built locomotive to run on steam. Cooper built this locomotive for the Baltimore & Ohio Railroad to convince the owners to change from horse-drawn carriages to steam-powered locomotives. The *Tom Thumb* raced, and lost, against a horse-drawn car. However, the demonstration was successful enough that the owners decided to start using steam engines. (Baltimore & Ohio Railroad Museum.)

As the first stone masonry bridge built for an American railroad, the Carrollton Viaduct (1828–1829) is located just inside the Baltimore city line and is the first major span the railroad crossed. Named for Charles Carroll of Carrollton, the last living signer of the Declaration of Independence, the viaduct is still in use today, carrying far heavier loads than ever envisioned by its builders. (Library of Congress.)

VIADUCT ON BALTIMORE & WASHINGTON RAILROAD

The next major crossing south from Baltimore was over the Patapsco River. Built from 1833 to 1835 and designed by Benjamin Henry Latrobe II, the Thomas Viaduct was named for the Baltimore & Ohio Railroad's first president. At the time of completion, the viaduct was the largest curved stone bridge in the United States and remains the oldest multi-arched stone bridge still in service. (Library of Congress.)

In this engraving, four coaches and a steam locomotive scare off two cows as the train approaches modern Washington, DC. Entitled *Tiber Creek, Northeast of the Capital*, this image pictures an area roughly in Ivy City or Brentwood, within the Washington, DC, boundaries. In the distance, the hills would be where the Bladensburg or Hyattsville stations would have been located. (Library of Congress.)

Relay House, above, was built in 1830 as the stop where horses would be changed for the six miles to Ellicott City. Serving as a hotel and train station, the building was used until 1872, when a new Victorian building was constructed where the tracks split. Today, Relay House is a private residence. The 1872 hotel was built very near the Builders Monument. The 15-foot stone obelisk shown at left contains the name of the builder of the Thomas Viaduct, the directors of the railroad, and the architect/engineer. Lead builder John McCartney "baptized" the Thomas Viaduct here by having his laborers kneel on the tracks and pour a pint of whiskey over their heads. The monument still stands, though it is often a target for graffiti. (Above, New York Public Library; left, Baltimore & Ohio Railroad Museum.)

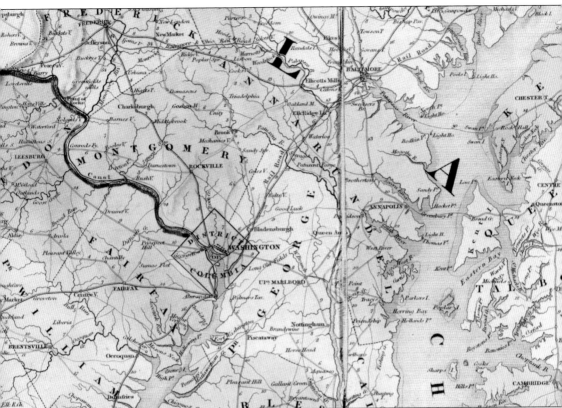

This detail from *The American Atlas* shows the distances on the Baltimore-to-Washington Turnpike and the parallel Baltimore & Ohio Railroad. Also shown is a four-pointed District of Columbia. Howard County is missing, having not yet been established. Fully entitled *The American Atlas, Exhibiting the Post Offices, Post Roads, Rail Roads, Canals, and the Physical and Political Divisions of the United States of North America* and published in 1839, this atlas and map document life in the region before the Civil War. Elkridge Landing, Waterloo, Savage, Beltsville, and Bladensburg, with an H, are all visible. Also note the Chesapeake & Ohio Canal paralleling the Potomac River and that Washington was a separate town within the District of Columbia. (Library of Congress.)

Samuel F.B. Morse supported himself through much of his life as a painter. However, in 1825, he received a message by horseman alerting him that his wife had become deathly ill. By the next day, a new message arrived that she had died. He returned from Washington, DC, to his home in New Haven, Connecticut, to find his wife was already buried. This spurred Morse to find a method for quick, long-distance communication. In 1832, he submitted a patent for the electromagnetic telegraph. Ten years later, Congress appropriated $30,000 for a line between Washington, DC, and Baltimore using the railroad right-of-way. Riversdale, shown below in the early 1900s, was where Morse did some testing, trying connections between Bladensburg and Beltsville. Morse transmitted his famous "What hath God wrought" message in 1844 over these lines. (Both, Library of Congress.)

The transmission of telegraphic signals could not be accomplished without the wires and poles that were central to the creation of the telegraph system. These two images from the 1850s show the landscape of the telegraph lines. Ezra Cornell, later the founder of Cornell University, invented a plow that would dig a ditch, lay pipes with the telegraph lines inside, and cover the ditch back up. However, it was soon discovered that the wires quickly became wet, shorting out. He then created a solution—the glass insulator—to allow lines to be hung from "700 straight and sound chestnut posts with the bark on and . . . not less than eight inches in diameter . . . tapering to five or six inches at the top . . . to be 24 feet in length." (Above, Library of Congress; right, National Archives and Records Administration.)

CAMP CASEY, NEAR BLADENSBURG, M?

4TH REGT. R.I.V. COL.J.P. RADMAN.   5TH REGT. N.H.V. COL. EDWARD CROSS.

The Civil War began at Fort Sumter in South Carolina in 1860, ripping the nation in half. Washington, DC, was located between Virginia, a Confederate state, and Maryland, a state with mixed loyalties. Prince George's County leaned heavily toward the Confederate cause because of the strong plantation system the county relied on for income. This meant that Washington had to have significant fortifications to protect the city from the surrounding areas. Fort Lincoln was established in 1861 with the Baltimore-to-Washington Road to the north and Bladensburg to the east. Camp Casey, the large parade and training grounds, was located just outside the fortifications in modern Colmar Manor. Laurel Factory, Annapolis Junction, and Relay were all heavily fortified, ensuring safe passage along the rail line. By the end of the Civil War in 1865, Washington was the most heavily fortified city in the United States, with 68 forts, 807 mounted cannons, and miles of roads, telegraph lines, and buildings encircling the city. (Library of Congress.)

As one of the many fortifications, Fort Lincoln's primary job was to protect the Baltimore-to-Washington Turnpike and the Baltimore & Ohio Railroad where the roads crossed into Washington, DC. Two major batteries were located outside the Washington line, and some evidence of them remains in the Fort Lincoln Cemetery, where there was a 100-pounder and four 20-pounder cannons as well as other artillery pieces. The 4th US Colored Infantry Regiment was positioned at Fort Lincoln in November 1865, after the end of the Civil War, as shown below. The regiment was initially mustered in Baltimore and served in a variety of locations, especially North Carolina. It was assigned to the Department of North Carolina but was eventually positioned at the Defenses of Washington as part of that assignment. (Both, Library of Congress.)

Traveling north on the road or railroad, troops would arrive at the Muirkirk Iron Works, shown above with the Baltimore & Ohio Railroad in the foreground. Established in 1847, the Muirkirk Works were considered one of the finest at the time and advertised "the strongest pig iron in the United States." Iron would be used for artillery by Union manufacturers. During the Civil War, many of the laborers came from the nearby freedmen's community of Rossville. North of Muirkirk was Camp Kelsey at Annapolis Junction. The engraving below shows the festivities around Thanksgiving, with the Baltimore & Ohio rail line in the foreground. Two long lines of tents for the 10th Maine, Company F, flank a large table filled with food from their "friends in Lewiston." (Above, Maryland–National Capital Park and Planning Commission; below, Library of Congress.)

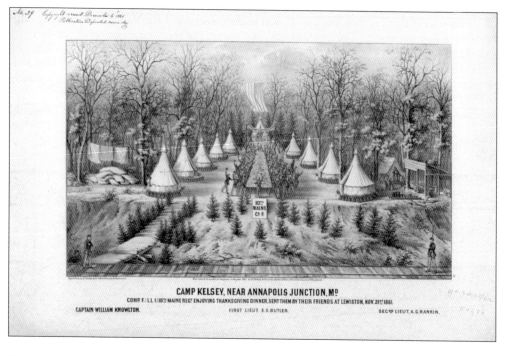

CAMP KELSEY, NEAR ANNAPOLIS JUNCTION, M?

COMP. F.I LL. I) 10?? MAINE REG? ENJOYING THANKSGIVING DINNER, SENT THEM BY THEIR FRIENDS AT LEWISTON, NOV. 21?? 1861.

CAPTAIN WILLIAM KNOWLTON.   FIRST LIEUT. E.S. BUTLER.   SEC?? LIEUT. A.G. RANKIN.

An actual sketch, made on the spot by one of the Special Artists of Frank Leslie's Illustrated Newspaper.

Mr. Leslie holds the copyright and reserves the exclusive right of publication.

Boston Battery at General Butler's camp, Relay House. ... the Balt. & Ohio railroad & Patapsco river

Another engraving from the Civil War, this one from *Leslie's Illustrated Weekly* (above), shows an entrenchment on the rail line at Relay. The caption notes "the battery at General Butler's camp, Relay House, covering the Balto & Ohio Railroad and Patapsco River." These cannons would be aimed toward the Thomas Viaduct. Union leaders recognized the importance of this bridge for supplies coming to and from Washington, DC. Aimed the other direction, the soldiers in the stereoscopic view below have formed an entrenchment on the hillside now known as Lawyer's Hill. This hill above the rail line was home to many Southern sympathizers but was now filled with Union troops. After the war finished, a local judge donated land to create the Elkridge Assembly Room to "heal any separations" within the neighborhood. (Both, Library of Congress.)

After the Civil War, many of the communities along the Washington-to-Baltimore route—either by train or by cart—returned to a quiet life. These views of the Elkridge Station (above) and the Annapolis Junction Station (below) show rural landscapes waiting patiently for the arrival of the hourly trains. Both stations display a level of Victorian architectural detail. The Annapolis Junction Hotel, in the center of the image below, retains a more traditional feel, while the newer freight building to the left exhibits some Victorian Gothic detailing. This is the point where the Annapolis & Elk Ridge would have split off to travel toward Annapolis across the modern Fort Meade. The Annapolis & Elk Ridge would eventually be closed to regular train traffic and be replaced by the Washington, Baltimore & Annapolis interurban trolley line. (Above, Elkridge Heritage Society; below, Southern Methodist University.)

Taken at the same time as the Annapolis Junction image, these two photographs represent life in 1872 along the railroad. The Baltimore & Ohio Railroad had only increased in popularity since the Civil War, leaving the Baltimore-to-Washington Road nearly empty. The image above shows Laurel Mills from a position that is not commonly seen in historic images, capturing the length of the mill, then operated by George Nye. The site is now the location of the municipal pool. Bladensburg's rail station, shown below, was located at a distance from the actual downtown of Bladensburg. The station was approximately where Hyattsville's station would later be located, near the point where the Baltimore & Ohio Railroad crosses the turnpike. No train station ever existed within the historic town. (Both, Southern Methodist University.)

Located just north of Laurel and south of Annapolis Junction, Savage Mill was a major cotton mill near the Baltimore & Ohio and the Baltimore-to-Washington Road. As a manufacturer of sailcloth, the mill was established in 1821 and was known to much of the country by 1825. By 1832, the mill had a gristmill, sawmill, machine shop, foundry, blacksmith shop, wheelwright, brick kiln, farms, rental houses, and a company store. In the 1870s, a Bollman truss bridge was constructed on the site, and it is now the only remaining example of this style of bridge in the United States. The 160-foot-long iron bridge was the first successful all-metal bridge using wrought iron tension members and cast iron compression members. (Above, New York Public Library; below, Howard County Historical Society.)

Manufacturing in the region was dependent on the rivers at places like Laurel and Savage. However, there has been a long history of iron working. Elkridge Furnace was one of the only industries that allowed the community to survive after the harbor had silted in. Meanwhile, the Muirkirk Iron Works, which had been so significant in the time of the Civil War, would ebb and flow in importance. The 1872 image below shows a very active worksite with piles of wood for use in the furnaces. While digging for iron in the area, a local scientist discovered the bones of the *Astrodon johnstoni*, now the Maryland state dinosaur. (Above, Maryland Highways Administration; below, Southern Methodist University.)

An 1884 advertisement for Viaduct Manufacturing reads, "having increased facilities, and ample capital, we will carry a large stock of telephone, telegraph, electric light . . . our works are on the Patapsco River, at the Relay Station, B & O RR with an abundance of water power. We carry continually, a large stock of cross-arms, pins, brackets, insulators, and wire." An 1890s ad says that the company "make everything electrical, but its specialties are telephones, magneto bells, district messenger call boxes, students telegraph outfit." Portions of the factory were built on the mill formerly at the site, which had necessitated the curve in the Thomas Viaduct. The owner of the company was A.G. Davis, a cousin of Samuel Morse, who had learned the telegraph trade in New York and Canada. (Both, Elkridge Heritage Society.)

AMERICAN SCENERY ———— THE INN ON THE ROADSIDE.

While the railroad was king from 1835 to the 1890s, there was still a bustling life along the roads, albeit a very local version. Long distance travel by cart was gone by the 1870s, when the transcontinental railroad was finished and much of the United States was bound together by steel rail. However, getting from the station to home still necessitated some travel. Additionally, gossip and news were still vital parts of the day-to-day life of those in the region. Thus the tavern remained an important part of the history of the roadside. Long since given up from the turnpike days of the Baltimore-to-Washington Road, the taverns along the route were now local meeting places. This image, *American Scenery—The Inn on the Roadside*, gives an impression of the life lived around these places. A Conestoga wagon is parked in front of the inn, perhaps indicating this inn is somewhere along the National Road headed for Pittsburgh and the Midwest. (Library of Congress.)

Bladensburg was one of the old towns bypassed by the railroad. A line was cut through in the 1870s without a stop in the center of the town. The only way to get into the old community was by cart from Hyattsville or the road to Annapolis. This image of the Palo Alto Tavern in 1899 shows a historic old building that may have a unique claim to fame. Located across from the modern George Washington House, the Palo Alto was reported in 1908 to be the birthplace of a cocktail created after a duel at the dueling grounds. To the north, buried under a modern pumping station, is the former Spa Spring. The natural spring's waters were noted for medicinal properties. Doctors sent Washington, DC, politicians here to take the waters. (Both, Prince George's County Historical Society.)

North from Bladensburg, the Rossborough Inn took on a new life after the road became a turnpike. Built by Richard Ross around 1803 and decorated by a Coade keystone made in London in 1798, the building was serving as a tavern in 1812, when the road became a turnpike. George Calvert of Riversdale purchased the Rossborough (or Rossburg) property in 1821, and it was during his ownership that Lafayette and his retinue spent the night in the tavern during the general's visit in 1824. A generation later, in 1858, Calvert's son, an enthusiastic supporter of agricultural education, conveyed the Rossburg Farm to the newly incorporated Maryland Agricultural College. Focus at the school was on scientific and practical agriculture and included an experimental and model farm built around the inn. The Maryland Agricultural College would later become the University of Maryland. In 1937–1938, the Works Progress Administration was involved in "restoring" the building, which meant completely changing the roofline and gutting the building. (University of Maryland Special Collections.)

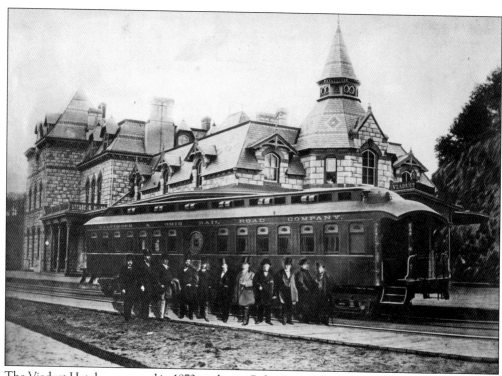

The Viaduct Hotel was opened in 1872, replacing Relay House. The hotel was placed in a triangular portion of land at the middle of the wye junction. This large Gothic building was a combination hotel, restaurant, and train station designed by railroad architect Francis Baldwin. The building included multicolored slate roof tiles with rows of brownstone and Patapsco granite for the walls. The restaurant portion had a dining room and bar, while behind the building was an English garden with a pathway to the river. Small rooms were available for single nights, but the hotel was not intended for long-term stays. By 1938, the building was taken out of use as faster trains sped by, and it was torn down in 1950. (Above, Baltimore Public Library at Catonsville; below, Elkridge Heritage Society.)

Three

TRAINS, TROLLEYS, AND PLANES ALONG ROUTE 1

1890–1930

At the dawn of the 20th century, railroads remained firmly in control. However, the transportation landscape along the old Baltimore-to-Washington Road would soon change drastically with the arrival of trolleys, automobiles, and soon, the airplane. This 1902 image shows dignitaries, the mayor, and city council at the end of the City & Suburban trolley line in Laurel for an "inspection trip" to Washington. (National Capital Trolley Museum.)

THE TWENTIETH CENTURY F

WRIGHT AEROPLANE.

Nothing represented the changes to transportation at the start of the 20th century more noticeably than the arrival of the airplane, here physically and figuratively overtaking the older methods of travel. In this postcard from College Park in 1909 ("COPR 1909"), a brand-new Wright Aeroplane, just taking off from the US Army airfield, is flying over the Baltimore & Ohio Railroad. This "Twentieth Century Flyer" was representational of how technologies were changing the American landscape of transportation and travel. Visible along the railroad are telegraph and telephone poles,

ER" "COPR" 190 SEABROOK BROS 906 F ST

linking the nation together through communications. Meanwhile, just a few hundred feet away, new automobiles are running on the old Baltimore-to-Washington Road, now called the Atlantic Highway but soon to be State Highway 1. The corridor between Washington and Baltimore was becoming ground zero for major advances in transportation. Economic changes from agriculture to an economy dependent on the federal government workforce, such as the Army, meant that communities and residents had to change too. (College Park Aviation Museum.)

In this photograph from 1900, a Baltimore & Ohio Railroad locomotive is under power near Laurel. Five coaches long, the daily train between Washington and Baltimore was filled with commuters and travelers headed further abroad. However, the economics of railroading were changing, and the Baltimore & Ohio would be acquired by the Pennsylvania Railroad in the coming year. (Baltimore & Ohio Railroad Museum.)

"Train of the Future" read the headline on July 10, 1900. Frederick Adams of Chicago used the Washington line to test his theory of streamlining trains with the *Windsplitter*. "Instead of being a series of connected boxes on wheels, it will have graceful and continuous lines," reads the report. His first test reached 90 miles per hour, significantly faster than other trains at the time (Baltimore & Ohio Railroad Museum.)

A few miles distant from the Baltimore & Ohio line was the Pennsylvania line. The community of Huntington is shown here at the point where the lines diverged to Popes Creek or Washington in the late 1800s, just after the Pennsylvania used a little-known loophole in the rules to reach into Washington, DC. Today, the community is known as "Old Bowie." (City of Bowie Museums.)

Hyattsville had one of the grander stations along the Baltimore & Ohio Railroad. Shown here in the mid-1910s, the station was located just about where US Route 1 met Rhode Island Avenue. The station was built in 1884 with a design by Francis Baldwin, the railroad's main architect. The building was demolished in the 1950s. (Prince George's County Historical Society.)

This photograph brings many different parts of the history of transportation together in one image at a golden time of rail development. Riverdale Park is where transportation methods began to meet. Trains continued to serve commuters, while trolleys provided access to intermediate stops along the route. A Baltimore & Ohio Railroad locomotive under steam sits in front of the Riverdale Park station. In the background to the left is the City & Suburban trolley running toward Laurel from Washington, while behind the church, farther left, is the Baltimore-to-Washington Road. Crossing the tracks in the foreground is modern Queensbury Road. Today, this wide-open landscape has been transformed with the Town Center shops. The trolley line has been replaced by a hiker/biker trail, while the railroad line is now a commuter rail line. In the rear of the scene is where the modern East-West Highway bridge is now located. (Prince George's County Historical Society.)

Starting with this blurry picture taken while in motion, the next few photographs will present a tour of the rail line toward Elkridge utilizing images from a survey for the Interstate Commerce Commission. This station is Brentwood. No other photograph of the station has ever been identified. The station is a standard building style for the Baltimore & Ohio Railroad. To the right is the freight shed. (Baltimore & Ohio Railroad Museum.)

Viewed to the south, this image shows the US Route 1 grade crossing in Hyattsville. This grade crossing was closed in 1929 and replaced by a viaduct. On the left, high above the track is the guard station that controlled the crossing gate. Behind the guard station is the Hyattsville station. To the right, behind the platform, telephone poles mark the trolley line. (Prince George's County Historical Society.)

Farther up the line, after Riverdale Park and College Park, was Branchville. In this image from 1900, Branchville is a modern and new station along the railroad. This location is roughly along Greenbelt Road, just north of Berwyn. Today, the location is an industrial park and Metro line. (Baltimore & Ohio Railroad Museum.)

Continuing north is the Contee station. Again, the design is a standard Baltimore & Ohio Railroad design, with the passenger station on the left and a freight house on the right. This location would be considered south Laurel today. Contee Road retains the name, and the station would have been just a block from US Route 1. (Baltimore & Ohio Railroad Museum.)

Crossing into Howard County, the large Jessup station was set a mile away from US Route 1 on the mainline of the railroad. This station shows architectural details often left off smaller stations, with gingerbread molding and a steep, peaked roof. Stations like these were often the hub of the community, with residents coming to collect freight, news, and gossip. The Dorsey station, which was the next station heading north, is shown below. The freight house is to the left with the station behind. On the left is the Wells Fargo & Co. Express building for shipping. Based on the materials on the porch, the building appears to also serve as a general store and post office. (Both, Baltimore & Ohio Railroad Museum.)

Prior to 1908, this intersection near Elkridge would have been a deeply rutted, barely maintained road. The house in the background still stands. Montgomery Road, which still exists, leads toward Ellicott City and the National Pike, or US Route 40. This photograph, taken in the first decade of the 20th century, was part of the documentation for new improvements installed by the state roads commission. Established with the goal of constructing a state road system, the commission was loaned $5 million to begin work in 1910. Later merged with the existing state highway department in the state geological survey, this new commission began analyzing all the roads in the state and developed a work plan to make roads usable. This survey showed that there was significant demand for a good road between Baltimore and Washington and a need to upgrade the National Pike. (Maryland State Archives.)

Automobiles required special skills to repair. That meant that a new trade had to be learned quickly, and one of the best qualified to learn that skill was the village blacksmith. With tools and the skills to fabricate new parts, the blacksmith was well prepared for the innovation. "Casey the blacksmith" in Bladensburg (above), or this unidentified blacksmith in Laurel (below), were common to the time. Casey has a large range of old wheels and axles strewn around the building, while the Laurel smithy shows a slightly neater interior. (Above, Prince George's County Historical Society; below, Library of Congress.)

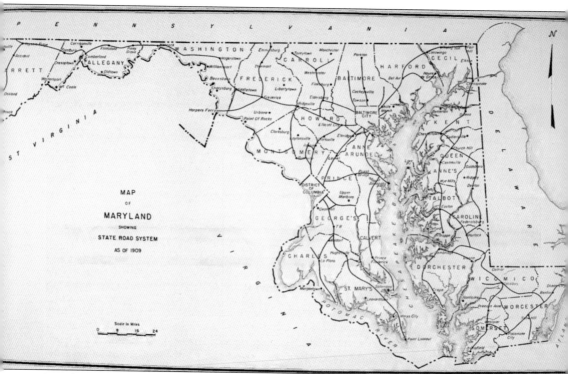

Maryland was a changing and growing landscape for cars in the early 20th century. The state roads commission surveyed the roads and provided maintenance to primary roads. This map from a 1909 report to the legislature shows the extent to which the state had been making efforts to label and organize major routes. Connecting routes were made from Washington, DC, to Baltimore, Point Lookout, and Annapolis. Connecting routes from Baltimore included to Frederick westward and Havre de Grace eastward on what would be modern US Route 40. US Route 1, or State Highway 1 as it was known then, is shown clearly passing from Washington to Laurel and then Elkridge. The old route between Bladensburg and Annapolis, now modernized to become Maryland Route 450, is shown passing through Priest Bridge, approximately where Bowie is today. (Maryland Highways Administration.)

Part of the development of Maryland's modern roads was born out of the Good Roads Movement. Started by bicyclists in the 1880s, the goal was to create safe roads for cyclists and for rural communities. Advocates used images like the one above to influence politicians to improve roads. By 1916, President Wilson signed the Federal Aid Road Act into law as an effort to support road construction, now more for cars than bicycles. Below, President Coolidge meets with the advocates in 1924 to expand the work. Maryland was ahead of that curve by starting the state roads commission in 1904. (Both, Library of Congress.)

Automobiles were a growing industry as the roads improved. The Hyattsville Automobile Company was one of the first Ford dealerships in Prince George's County. Located at the corner of Emerson Street and Baltimore Avenue (now Alternate Route 1), the building began as a livery stable. With the switch to automobiles, a large gas pump was installed, and inside, the building was painted white to reflect more light for workers. Below, the owner or manager smiles over the workers hard at their labor. To the right are the remains of the box stalls that kept the horses before the automobiles arrived. The scene is not much different than in today's repair shops. The picture above is from 1909, while the picture below is from 1927. (Both, Library of Congress.)

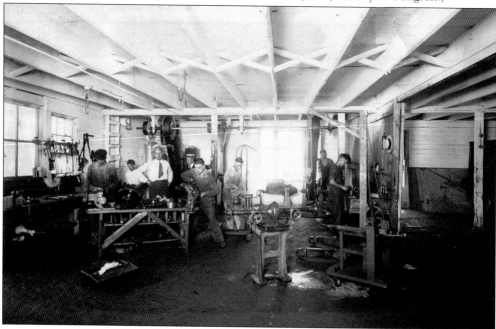

Nearby, the Carter Motor Car Company established its factory in a large building (above). Gary and Frank Carter started the company in 1907 to build the Washington Roadster, available for $1,250. Their advertisement said "the car is constructed of the best material throughout. We back this statement with an ironclad guarantee." The factory was listed in Hyattsville, located in what is now the industrial section of Edmonston. The sales room was in downtown Washington, DC. Community leaders in Berwyn tried unsuccessfully to lure the factory, but the Carters selected Edmonston because of the closer proximity to the highways and trains. As quickly as the car came, the company went into bankruptcy in 1912 and dissolved by 1917. (Both, Library of Congress.)

While the automobile was gaining on the trains, another form of travel was connecting small towns throughout the US Route 1 corridor. The trolley, or streetcar as it was known locally, could provide quick, clean service without the long distances of train travel. Streetcars started in Washington, DC, as early as 1862 but did not become commonplace until the 1880s with the introduction of electric power. In 1890, the City & Suburban Railway was chartered to run from the Treasury Building to Mount Rainier at the Washington boundary. However, no streetcars would travel along the line until 1897. In 1898, a City & Suburban Railway car is pictured under construction prior to installation on the new line. Shortly thereafter, the Maryland & Washington Railway was incorporated in Maryland to connect this line to Branchville and Laurel. Within four years, the lines merged, along with several other companies, to create the Columbia & Maryland Railway. (National Capital Trolley Museum.)

This image shows a streetcar arriving at Mount Rainier about where Rhode Island Avenue would be built. These tracks were built into Mount Rainier in 1897, reached Brentwood and North Brentwood in 1898, and finally arrived in Hyattsville in 1899. There was also an attempt to build a line south from Baltimore to parallel US Route 1 to Washington, DC, but the construction never went farther than Ellicott City. (National Capital Trolley Museum.)

The Columbia & Maryland Railway was renamed the Berwyn & Laurel Electric Railroad Company around 1900. Construction built toward Riverdale, College Park, Beltsville, and Laurel, arriving in 1902. Once the tracks reached Laurel, the company was again renamed, this time to the Washington, Berwyn & Laurel Electric Railroad. This photograph shows a streetcar in Hyattsville in the 1940s. (National Capital Trolley Museum.)

At Riverdale Park, this streetcar, painted in Washington Railway & Electric Company (WRECo) colors, sits next to town center shops and the Baltimore & Ohio station in 1935. WRECo was the company that absorbed the Washington, Berwyn & Laurel. WRECo was then absorbed into the new Capital Transit. The streetcar is headed inbound to the Treasury Building. Note the overhead wire and pickup configuration. (National Capital Trolley Museum.)

A Capital Transit streetcar glides through College Park in 1939 running northbound. This part of the route is known today as Rhode Island Avenue between Branchville Road and US Route 1 in Beltsville, where the wide road in the middle is flanked by service roads leading into the neighborhoods. The 82 on the streetcar was the number for the entire route to Laurel. (National Capital Trolley Museum.)

Crossing US Route 1 at Beltsville, this Capital Transit trolley is headed southbound. The sharp angle of the crossing is still evident today. By 1945, Capital Transit had the third largest streetcar fleet in the United States. Many residents from the time remember taking the streetcar into the city. Streetcars were a vital part of living in the southern part of the US Route 1 corridor. (National Capital Trolley Museum.)

Employees of the streetcar fleet stand in the center doorway of a Laurel-bound trolley. Motormen tended to have longer jackets, while conductors wore coin changer machines. District of Columbia regulations required two men operating the car, while Maryland allowed for only one. This photograph was likely taken at the Eckington Car House at Third and T Streets NE in Washington, DC. (National Capital Trolley Museum.)

The Annapolis & Elk Ridge Railroad branched from the Baltimore & Ohio Railroad at Annapolis Junction. Construction started in 1838, and service began in 1840. The route ran from Annapolis via Crownsville, Millersville, and Odenton before connecting with the main line. Having served for 60 years, the line was purchased in 1902 by the new Washington, Baltimore & Annapolis Railway to create an interurban, or electric powered railway. Paralleling the Pennsylvania Railroad line and crossing the Annapolis & Elk Ridge at Odenton, the railway provided service to Annapolis. This proved vital when World War I broke out and the US Army set up a camp in an area bounded by the Baltimore & Ohio, the Pennsylvania, and the Washington, Baltimore & Annapolis Railways. This camp is now known as Fort Meade. (Both, National Capital Trolley Museum;.)

Fort Meade was a major part of the story of US Route 1. Initially opened as Camp Admiral in 1917, the 30-square-mile camp was home to the Field Signal School and the Camp Benning tank school. More than 400,000 soldiers passed through the site from 1917 to 1919 while training for World War I. During the 1917–1918 period, over 8.5 million passengers traveled by train or trolley to the site. Additionally, over 22,000 horses and mules were brought to the camp during World War I to service the remount station. Remount soldiers were tasked with training and maintaining the animals for service on the front lines. Freight service was critical to the new camp, bringing construction supplies, coal, and even flour and sugar for the Cooks and Bakers School. (Both, Library of Congress.)

Fort Meade and World War I had a major impact on the needs for infrastructure, goods, animals, and troops necessary to achieve the surge of soldiers fighting in Europe. These two images give a sense of scale of the operation at Fort Meade. The picture above shows the teams of horses necessary to pull supply carts. Several dozen barns and paddocks can be seen, while in the distance are barracks and offices. Below, a different vehicle is evident—the automobile. Large trucks and motorcycles can be seen on the far left, ready for service. Brand new barracks are being put up hastily to provide housing for the thousands of trainees. Unfortunately, many of these men would never return from the battles. (Both, Library of Congress.)

After World War I, soldiers returned to their lives during the Roaring Twenties. However, the jubilation was short lived, as the Great Depression came after the stock market crash of 1929. This image shows workers returning from a day at the Resettlement Administration's Berwyn Project, now Greenbelt, and walking alongside the Baltimore & Ohio Railroad tracks. The station is on the far right in the distance. (Library of Congress.)

Trains continued to dominate travel during the 1920s and 1930s. Long-distance travel on the *Royal Blue* was the height of luxury, here crossing the Thomas Viaduct. The name was reintroduced in 1935 for the route from Washington, DC, to New York. However, the line ended just over 20 years later as passenger service declined due to the automobile. (Baltimore & Ohio Railroad Museum.)

In 1903, the Wright brothers defied gravity and launched the first American airplane at Kitty Hawk, North Carolina. Over four years, the Wright brothers negotiated and courted the US Army to take on one of their airplanes. The Wright brothers were required to train the flyers as well. The first school was set up at Fort Myers, Virginia. However, the location proved to be too small and too popular. During a balloon ascent, Lt. Frank Lahm spotted the College Park site. Easily accessible by train, trolley, and automobile, the site was hoped to be far enough away from Washington, DC, to provide a level of privacy. This photograph shows a variety of hangars from the Calvert Road side of the airfield. The first few hangars were for a private airplane builder, while the four rounded hangars at right were for the Army. (College Park Aviation Museum.)

When Wilbur Wright came to College Park in October 1909, he brought the latest developments for testing and training. One of the key parts of the launch system was the use of a monorail, which was required before the use of landing wheels. The very early image above shows military flyers loading the airplane onto the track for launching. Below, soldiers and Army flyers hoist the remains of an airplane that has just crashed. They march past the Rex Smith Aeroplane Company hangar. Today, the field is still in use, but the main runway has been turned 90 degrees from the runway in use in 1909. The College Park Airport is the oldest continuously operating airfield in the world. (Above, College Park Aviation Museum; below, Library of Congress.)

In August 1918, the Post Office Department began airmail service between College Park and New York. The photograph above shows pilot Max Miller and representatives from the Post Office loading mail for this initial flight. However, the flights out of College Park closed just three years later, when the service moved to New York for a transcontinental route. Navy commodore J.C. Gillmore and Lt. Thomas Milling are shown below flying a Curtiss plane. Gilmore would retire in a few years, but Lieutenant Milling went on to become General Milling and helped push for the creation of a stand-alone air force. College Park's field is unique in the variety of special moments that have happened there, earning it the name "Field of Firsts." (Above, College Park Aviation Museum; below, Library of Congress.)

Queen's Chapel Airport in Hyattsville opened in the 1930s just beyond the Hamilton Street and Queen's Chapel Road intersection. By the time of this photograph in the 1940s, there were two hangars and two long, grass landing strips. However, by 1955, the site was closed and the Queen's Chapel Drive-In was opened with the "world's largest Cinemascope screen." (DC Public Library, Special Collections.)

In Greenbelt, William Schrom and his son Fritz operated a small airfield just beyond the center of town. Civilian pilot training programs used the field actively in the 1930s to train students from the University of Maryland. In its heyday, over 50 planes used the field on a regular basis. After World War II, the Civil Air Patrol used the field before the land was taken for housing and the Baltimore-Washington Parkway in 1954. (Greenbelt Museum.)

The Engineering and Research Corporation (ERCO) established its operations in Riverdale in 1937. Henry Berliner, who had worked on early helicopter prototypes at College Park, founded the company and worked to develop a variety of aviation items, the most famous being the Ercoupe airplane. The Civil Aeronautics Administration deemed the user-friendly plane "characteristically incapable of spinning." Berliner's lead designer and aeronautical engineer was Fred Weick, the innovator of many of the parts of the plane. The main factory building from 1939 is shown in the background above; it was torn down in 2015 for new development. Fred Weick is shown below in 1944 with the Ercoupe. (Both, College Park Aviation Museum.)

The 1945 aerial view above of the ERCO factory and airfield shows the size and scope of the changing landscape around the region. On the left is Calvert Homes, a large housing tract for ERCO employees during World War II building components for planes overseas. The airfield on the right was used for testing the Ercoupe. This location put the field just a few hundred yards away from the College Park airfield. In the center are the ERCO factory, the railroad right-of-way, and the trolley line. US Route 1 is just outside the image on the left. Below, the shop floor of the ERCO factory is filled with work in 1948, just a few years after retooling from the war effort. Note the female assembler at lower left. (Both, College Park Aviation Museum.)

Observation Ramp, Friendship Airport, Baltimore, Md.
Al Green Enterprises of Maryland, Inc.

The history of flight again took a major step forward in the region between Baltimore and Washington with the opening of Friendship Airport, now known as the Baltimore-Washington International Thurgood Marshall Airport. Friendship was dedicated in 1950 after a planning effort was made following World War II. The site was specifically chosen because the field would be on the Pennsylvania Railroad, the Baltimore & Annapolis interurban, and the newly planned Baltimore-Washington Parkway. The airport was dedicated by Pres. Harry Truman, who flew in from Washington National Airport. Using land purchased from a small church, the airport was built to be the only commercial jet service in the region. Until Washington Dulles was opened in 1962, this was the only airport near Washington that could accept transcontinental 707 flights. The airport was bought by the State of Maryland in 1972, and the name was changed to Baltimore-Washington International in 1973. The airport was the first to have a dedicated rail station for Amtrak, thus tying multiple strands of transportation together. (DC Public Library, Special Collections.)

Four

THE CHANGING FACE OF ROUTE 1

1930–1950

This long look northward up Route 1 from 1926 shows traffic coming from College Park toward Hyattsville. On the left is where the town of University Park would be built in a few short years. Traffic was heavy, even in these early days of the automobile. As more cars rolled out, there was an effort to develop the state roads commission to manage maintenance and construction. (National Archives and Records Administration.)

These two photographs, both from around 1920, show "Dead Man's Curve" about a mile south of Elkridge. Increasing traffic led to increasing accidents. With nearly 50 deaths and hundreds of accidents, the state roads commission sought to eliminate the curve in 1917. Previously, the road and embankment had been located to the left side of the image below, where the old poles still stand, completely obscuring the view around the curve at the top of the hill. The new alignment was still curved but opened the view and minimized the reversing curve, stemming the death toll. Yet, during the Prohibition, rumrunners still found the curves tricky, as reported in a 1924 *Baltimore Sun* article about a driver who "skidded at the curve and plunged over the 20-foot embankment." (Both, National Archives and Records Administration.)

Accidents along Route 1 ranged in type and severity. Just outside of College Park, near the fields of the Maryland Agricultural College, a woman and a small child peer into a car lying in the ditch. No one appears to be hurt, but the tire marks from the car still on the road seem to indicate that the accident had just happened and the car had come to a screeching halt. While one can only speculate on the reason for the accident, a report in *Public Roads: A Journal of Highway Research from 1921* by the Maryland state roads commissioner states that "the outstanding fact . . . is that the clear majority of the disasters that overtake motorists are brought upon themselves by their own recklessness, and 90 per cent are due to just one cause—speeding." At the same time, the state roads commission was adding larger shoulders, which might have kept this motorist from ending up in the ditch. The photograph is from 1932. (National Archives and Records Administration.)

A dump truck is lying in the Patuxent River after a bridge collapsed under its weight in 1924. Two men sit on the abutment, and a warning light is hung from wires to alert drivers. A massive structural failure like this is uncommon today, but poor construction techniques stymied early road builders. The state roads commission developed standards to combat this issue. (National Archives and Records Administration.)

This accident photograph from 1919 shows a large truck slammed into a telephone pole, destroying the truck, pole, and fence. Visible on the truck is a "Baltimore & Washington" sign, indicating the freight company route. Details of the type of freight are not visible, but the accident has drawn a crowd to this quiet stretch of Route 1. (National Archives and Records Administration.)

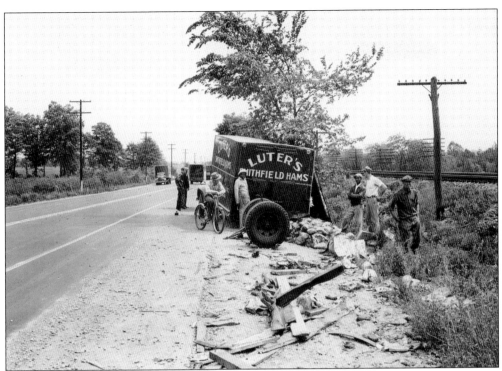

The freight being carried in this accident is much more obvious—Luter's Smithfield Hams. Taken in 1942 just north of Beltsville, where the road comes close to the Baltimore & Ohio Railroad right-of-way, the photograph shows hams spilling from the truck. The rear wheels and axle have been sheared off entirely. (National Archives and Records Administration.)

From time to time, trains met the cars, as seen here in 1936. This photograph shows the remains of an automobile destroyed by a large locomotive, now derailed. The crowd is all smiles for the photographer, but the interior of the car looks much more serious. The No. 1474 Baltimore & Ohio locomotive was built in 1909, rebuilt in 1926, and scrapped in 1947. (National Archives and Records Administration.)

As Route 1 and the automobile grew in dominance, surpassing the railroads and trolleys, roads had to be rebuilt to support the growing population. State reports from 1918 indicate that trucks used for World War I were often oversized for the roads, destroying the subsurface. This photograph shows a work crew spreading bitumen (tar) in 1915, a common method for treating the roads at the time. However, within a few short years, Maryland's state roads commission embarked on a large project to install concrete shoulders and better graded main roads. By 1920, the state had spent $30 million on roads around the state. This photograph also documents the Washington, Spa Spring & Gretta trolley line just outside of Bladensburg. Almost no history remains of this line. The exact location near Bladensburg cannot be determined with accuracy because the landscape has changed so much. (National Archives and Records Administration.)

Workers in 1918 oversee a large concrete machine. Concrete was used for shoulders, while the center was macadam or blacktop. Oiling cans are lined up along the side of the road at this location just north of Laurel. Roads were regraded to have a lower crown in the center, and the shoulders provided a smoother passing location. This appears to be an integrated work crew. (National Archives and Records Administration.)

Taken near the Maryland Agricultural College, this photograph from 1921 demonstrates the changing users of Route 1. Walkers simply use the middle of the road, while cars and horse-drawn wagons intermingle. Piles of material are stacked along the sides ready for patching. A report from 1918 notes that these piles of patching material would be laid out in fall to be ready for spring work. (National Archives and Records Administration.)

Flooding was common in Bladensburg, Laurel, and Elkridge, where the rivers ran close to the highway. Above, the flooding of the Anacostia River reaches into Bladensburg, where cars have to run through the water. However, much of Bladensburg's residential area was on the hills leading toward Cheverly and Annapolis, so damage was limited. In the image below, the other side of the river did not fare as well. On the left is modern Cottage City, while on the right is modern Colmar Manor. In the far distance is the Peace Cross and bridge. The river would flood like this nearly every year until the Army Corps of Engineers developed major levees along the river in the 1920s. None of the buildings in either image remain except the Peace Cross. (Above, Library of Congress; below, National Archives and Records Administration.)

The Patapsco River was no different in flooding. During the hurricane of 1933, which damaged much of the Chesapeake region, the flooding reached a 100-year high. Buildings were damaged or destroyed, roads washed out, and property was destroyed. As shown above, Elkridge appears devastated just after the massive flooding washed through the area. Similarly, in 1972, Hurricane Agnes ripped through the area. Trees and mud filled the Patapsco River at the Thomas Viaduct, as seen below. Looking downstream (Relay is to the left), the 1835 stone structure is still as strong today and has withstood many major floods and hurricanes. (Both, Elkridge Heritage Society.)

With images from the Bureau of Public Roads collection mixed with a few from the Library of Congress and the DC Public Library, a ride through history from the Washington, DC, line to the Baltimore city line can be constructed. Starting in Bladensburg, Cottage City, and Colmar Manor, US Route 1 leaves Washington headed north. Here is where the docks for Bladensburg, the famous dueling grounds, and the Battle of Bladensburg were all located. As shown in this early 1900s image, the Memorial Cross, now called the Peace Cross, was built to honor the soldiers killed in World War I. The American Legion in Hyattsville took over the project, which was half finished at this point in history. To the left appears to be the road into Bladensburg. The white wall on the right forms the end of the bridge to Washington. This marker will be the starting point for a journey along US Route 1. (DC Public Library, Washington Star Collection.)

This image shows where modern Maryland 450 meets Maryland 202 near the Bladensburg and Cheverly town lines. This intersection continues to be busy today, but the landscape has changed much. Just beyond the image to the right is the Cheverly Theater, now the Publick Playhouse. The caption from the *Washington Star* indicates that this photograph shows the traffic returning from the beaches. (DC Public Library, Washington Star Collection.)

In this view looking south toward Cottage City and Colmar Manor, US Route 1 heads back into Washington, DC. Telephone poles make scraggly lines along the bridge over the Anacostia River. Large billboards cover both sides of the road. Advertising for Olmsted Grill beckons drivers to the city's largest dining room, famous for oysters. A stone wall, which no longer exists, surrounds the Peace Cross. (National Archives and Records Administration.)

Main Street, looking South, Hyattsville, Md.

US Route 1, in this view southward in 1928, has just crossed the railroad line to the left of the image. Listed as "Main Street," this part of the road was always known as Maryland Avenue or Baltimore Avenue. Large awnings, neon signs, and plenty of on-street parking were common in 1928. Just to the right by the dentist would be the silent movie theater and bowling alley known as the Arcade. In the northbound view below, taken from roughly the same point, is the commercial strip of Hyattsville, much of which has disappeared. On the left is Woolworths, Peoples Drug Store, and the Federal Diner. The Woolworth building remains today. In the distance is what is known today as the Verizon Building, missing the extra three stories that were built later. (Both, National Archives and Records Administration.)

Looking back toward Bladensburg from Hyattsville, this overpass was built in the late 1920s to eliminate the grade crossing of the Baltimore & Ohio Railroad. In this view, the overpass heads toward a large hill in the distance where the Prince George's Hospital Center in Cheverly stands today. On the right is the Hyattsville Hardware Store. The three-story building remains today as part of Franklin's Restaurant. (National Archives and Records Administration.)

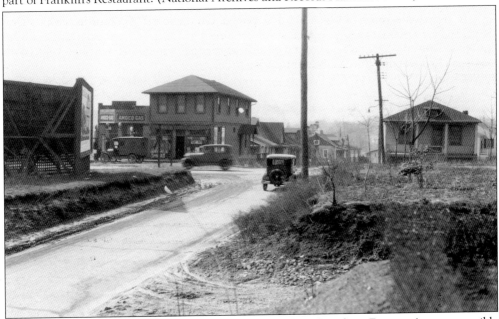

This view of the town of Mount Rainier in 1936 is believed to show Eastern Avenue, possibly crossing Rhode Island Avenue. Built in 1926 to parallel the streetcar line from Washington, DC, that route is now the primary route of US Route 1. The old alignment was renumbered as Alternate US Route 1. Mount Rainier was named in 1891 after the famous mountain. (National Archives and Records Administration.)

After leaving Hyattsville, Route 1 passes Edmonston, Riverdale Park, and University Park before arriving in College Park. In the 1939 photograph above, two students are illegally crossing Route 1 toward the beer hall and bowling alley just south of the gates of the University of Maryland, seen in the center right rear of the image, slightly hidden by trees. The image below shows the opposite side of the street with more illegal crossings. In the center distance is the roof of Turner Hall, while to the right is an Esso station, the Maryland Book Exchange, and Albrecht's Pharmacy. The pharmacy block is now converted into several small restaurants and shops. Accidents from illegal pedestrian crossings finally forced the Maryland Highways Administration to erect barriers in 2015. (Both, National Archives and Records Administration.)

Other street scenes from the Bureau of Public Roads show College Park's streetside gas station, which was described as a business to be avoided. This Hudson dealership and College Park Auto Place is now Bentley's Restaurant, while the rounded glass block remains today as the Cornerstone Grill. In the background, the cleaner remains as a collection of shops including Third Eye Comics. (National Archives and Records Administration.)

In the center of College Park's business district was the Little Tavern, torn down in 2015 and replaced with a small park. This photograph, taken as part of the Maryland Historic Trust's inventory of historic places, shows the building in the 1980s. Founded in 1927 in Kentucky, the business became a regional chain by the 1930s. Only the Laurel building remains along this part of Route 1. (Maryland Historical Trust.)

Turning off Route 1 in the Berwyn neighborhood of College Park, a traveler would find a small community of houses, a US Post Office, an ice cream shop, and men waiting for the trolley that ran from Washington to Beltsville, just to the north. Farther east was the Berwyn Railroad station at the Baltimore & Ohio Railroad. Just beyond the tracks and a little north was the entrance point to the Berwyn Project, which would later be known as Greenbelt. The image below shows the muddy and rutted road just off Greenbelt Road that ran into the woods owned by the US government and home of the Berwyn Project. A guardhouse stands sentry at the entrance. (Both, Library of Congress.)

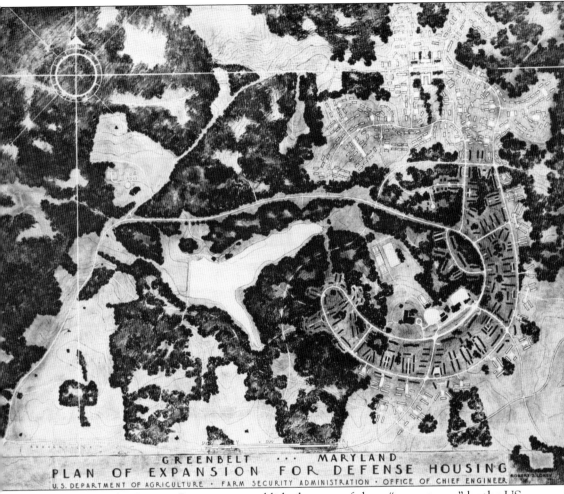

GREENBELT ··· MARYLAND
PLAN OF EXPANSION FOR DEFENSE HOUSING
U.S. DEPARTMENT OF AGRICULTURE · FARM SECURITY ADMINISTRATION · OFFICE OF CHIEF ENGINEER

Begun in 1935, the Berwyn Project was established as one of three "green towns" by the US government. These projects were intended to move people out of slum neighborhoods. Sites were established in Ohio, Wisconsin, and Maryland. A fourth was planned for New Jersey. Greenbelt, as the project became known, was designed around a natural ridge in a crescent pattern with the commercial and community center at the core surrounded by multifamily row houses. Homes were served by roads and parking on the "service side," while the "garden side" of the houses faced common pathways and gardens. Underpasses connected paths to the central movie theater, grocery, and shopping. Housing was initially rental-based and restricted by strict intake procedures. This map shows the plan for expanding the housing in the 1940s to accommodate defense workers. In 1953, the project was transferred into private ownership by a cooperative organization. Greenbelt is the only one of the three towns that retains the bulk of its original features, including the concept of cooperative ownership. (New York Public Library.)

Greenbelt quickly became a town for families. With underpasses that allowed children to ride without crossing major roads, families could be assured of safety. Separating cars from people was a vital part of the plan. Cars were kept to the edges or in specific routes that were at different levels than the interior pathways. Families could move from the playgrounds in the common areas to the large school at the center of the community without a car. However, cars could not be simply forgotten in the growing automobile landscape. The image below shows a carpool of government workers headed off for the day. Lines of carpools left from outside the apartment buildings in the background. Cars were necessary, since the project was not built with a connection to transit such as trains or trolleys. (Both, Library of Congress.)

The need for automobiles in Greenbelt was manifested in an auto repair shop and gas station, both of which were built on the side of the central commercial core. Known today as Roosevelt Center, this area with a large movie theater, a 5-and-10¢ store, a drugstore, city offices, and a fire station was where residents shopped and played. A gas station remains in the same location as the early gas station pictured above. Behind and to the left was the auto repair building. Also at Roosevelt Center was a place where residents could catch buses. The Greenbelt Line buses with their "Greenbelt Limited" placards shown below were the quickest way to get to the trolley at Berwyn or to the shopping in the surrounding area. (Both, Library of Congress.)

Cars and trucks stream by in this 1953 image of the Beltsville area. On the left is the Baltimore & Ohio Railroad, while on the right is the typical landscape of US Route 1 at the time. The Little Acres was a fried chicken restaurant, its large neon chick just barely visible behind the telephone poles in the center of the image. (National Archives and Records Administration.)

Entering Laurel, US Route 1 was greeted by a range of roadside eateries. Just behind the jaywalkers is the Little Tavern, which still stands today, advertising "excellent food" and "hamburgers 5¢." The little building is today a doughnut shop. Also visible is a wide variety of main street businesses, including the Laurel Pharmacy. (National Archives and Records Administration.)

This view from a slightly different angle gives a glimpse of the Laurel Diner before today's Tastee Diner. The diner appears in the center of this image. Opened in 1934, the first structure was a Silk City diner with end doors, which was uncommon. By 1951, the diner was moved out and replaced with the current diner. (National Archives and Records Administration.)

Continuing up the street, this image shows the Laurel Hotel, rooms "$1 per person." Steaks and chicken dinners, seafood, and cocktails for 25¢ were all advertised. Traffic was heavy through town, with Bish's Very Best Pies and Cakes leading the pack out of town and into Howard County. The building on the far right remains at the corner of Main Street and Baltimore Avenue. (National Archives and Records Administration.)

Leaving Laurel, US Route 1 rolls through the Savage area. Far removed from the industry around the railroad, this part of Savage was more rural and farm oriented. Here, billboards continue to clutter the road landscape, while in the distance is a Texaco and a small sign for Young's Hotel in the largest building at center. Note the wide concrete shoulders. (National Archives and Records Administration.)

This 1935 image shows a split in the road leading into Elkridge. The highway bypassed the older community of Elkridge in favor of a wide, smooth road that could be expanded on each side for the shoulders. The old road could not be expanded due to existing development. Note the fresh-cut hillside and the dirt road that was the original alignment for Route 1. (National Archives and Records Administration.)

This diner from Halethorpe is indicative of the type of small roadside diners that were common at the time. This was a site-built structure designed to look like a train car. A similar diner, Maxwell Diner, is visible in the center of the image below. Maxwell Diner, which included a dining room, can also be seen in an image in the Library of Congress mislabeled as a diner in Berwyn. The diner included an open-air portion featuring 25¢ platters, beer in frosted mugs, and hot dogs for 5¢, all at stools just steps from one's vehicle. While the underpass has changed in Elkridge, the rail line still crosses at this point on Route 1. (Right, Baltimore Public Library, Arbutus; below, National Archives and Records Administration.)

In a double set of images, a "time study" by the Bureau of Public Roads demonstrates changing landscapes. On the right is a photograph from 1927, while on the left is the same location in 1942. Certainly, wartime played a significant role in the reduced vehicle traffic; however, just as important are the widened road, the better shoulders, and the changed landscape. (National Archives and Records Administration.)

Another version of a comparative study is this photograph from 1953. Compare this with the image on page 77 at the beginning of this chapter to see how this part of the road landscape has changed. The community of University Park has sprung up, lights are installed, and US Route 1 is now a large four-lane road. Hidden by trees is a small guest house that remains today. (National Archives and Records Administration.)

As seen in many of the images from the Bureau of Public Roads, gas stations were vital parts of the roadside landscape of US Route 1. The Mobilgas station shown here at the corner of Forty-Second Place was common for the time. The image is labeled as Hyattsville, though the modern landscape has changed enough that identifying the exact location may be difficult. (National Archives and Records Administration.)

Similarly, this image, which shows the landscape just inside the Baltimore city limits in 1949, gives another look at the gas stations of the time. Sinclair, advertising Betholine, and Amoco were across from Esso stations. Hidden just behind the telephone poles and signs is the sign for a Howard Johnson's restaurant. The location appears to be Caton Avenue turning south toward Washington Boulevard. (National Archives and Records Administration.)

Compare these two images, taken in 1949 and 1961, showing the same stretch of US Route 1 in College Park. Both face north, looking toward Berwyn Road. On the left of the 1949 image are a variety of restaurants, billboards, gas stations, and even a frozen custard stand. On the right are more of the same, this time with a Tourist Cabin. A sign on the Sinclair station reads "student owned and operated." The 1961 image, on the other hand, has exploded with activity. A large Holiday Inn sign stands at the center rear, and signs for a wide range of diners, gas stations, car dealerships, and restaurants crowd the road. The Amoco appears to be in the same location. This image shows what many still consider to be the landscape of US Route 1. (Both, National Archives and Records Administration.)

In 1952, Alternate US Route 1 in Colmar Manor and Cottage City is a jumble of gas stations. On the left is Cottage City, not much changed today. The Tydol is still an auto repair building, and the cottages still exist. However, the Colmar Manor side is drastically different. The Peace Cross is not visible at this distance today due to a new bridge. (National Archives and Records Administration.)

George Laynor operated a gas station in Elkridge along US Route 1. An advertisement in the *Baltimore Sun* from 1924 lists him among those with Standard Ethyl Gas in Ellicott City, with his brother. Of course, these small-town gas stations were also places to get food or supplies. Signs in the store window advertise quality meats and groceries. (Elkridge Heritage Society.)

The One Spot Flea Killer dog was a major landmark along US Route 1. The building was the factory for One Spot Flea Killer until 1947 and was touted as the world's largest "dog house." It was covered with neon lights. An advertisement from the time stated that One Spot would "kill the fleas all over the animal from being applied only on one spot." (National Archives and Records Administration.)

Just as important as gas stations and restaurants were the motels. Del Haven White House bridged the eras of the Baltimore-to-Washington Road's use. Starting life as a tavern, the main building in the upper left served as a stopping point for generations. However, in the 20th century, the addition of a gas station and cottages brought new life as a cabin court. (Boston Public Library, Tichnor Brothers Collection.)

The Grand View Inn in Elkridge had cabins with showers and garages plus lunch and dining rooms, package goods, and liquors. The Tip Top Motor Court, below, and its grand sign still exist today. These motor court hotels were common along Route 1, providing quick places to stay on the travel up and down "America's Main Street." Cabin courts would transition to motels as buildings were pushed together or joined and converted into single buildings. Eventually, second stories were added, and the modern roadside motel was formed. A few old motels remain, with their single-level, cabin-court feel, especially in the area north of Laurel, formerly specializing as "no tell motels." The Valencia Motel near Laurel is one such example. (Above, Elkridge Heritage Society; below, Boston Public Library, Tichnor Brothers Collection.)

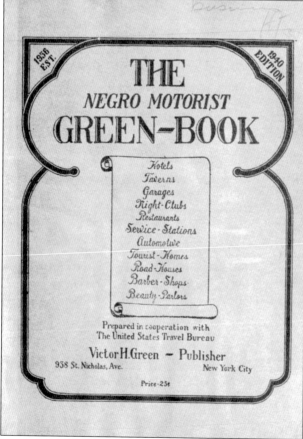

THE

NEGRO MOTORIST

GREEN-BOOK

1936 EST.

1940 EDITION

Hotels
Taverns
Garages
Night-Clubs
Restaurants
Service-Stations
Automotive
Tourist-Homes
Road-Houses
Barber-Shops
Beauty-Parlors

Prepared in cooperation with
The United States Travel Bureau

Victor H. Green — Publisher
958 St. Nicholas, Ave.   New York City

Price-25¢

The cabin courts, as shown above, were friendly locations with running water, heat, showers, and even chicken dinners. But motoring around the South was often a difficult situation for African American travelers. Victor Green published *The Negro Motorist Green-Book* to provide African American travelers the information and materials necessary to find resources for their travels. As his company wrote in the 1956 edition, "the white traveler has no difficulty in getting accommodations, but with the Negro it has been different. He, before the advent of a Negro travel guide, had to depend on word of mouth, and many times accommodations were not available." Unfortunately, not many sites along US Route 1 were listed in the *Green-Book*. (Above, Library of Congress; left, New York Public Library.)

Five

FROM ROADS TO ROCKETS
1950–1990

When World War II ended, the nation was in a time of boom. Nothing signaled the boom in the region more than the development of the Baltimore-Washington Parkway to replace US Route 1. Modern, sleek, and all new, the parkway and the developments between 1950 and today represented major shifts in transportation within the region. (National Archives and Records Administration.)

Train meets highway in this image showing a Baltimore & Ohio Railroad freight train gliding south past the Baltimore-Washington Parkway under construction in 1953. The railroads were struggling to stay relevant to a nation that preferred the private automobile to the passenger train. Meanwhile, the federal government was subsidizing new construction for automobiles at an increasing pace. (National Archives and Records Administration.)

The Pennsylvania Railroad was also attempting to stay ahead of the automobile. Shown here in 1954 is a GG-1 engine that ran on overhead electric wires. Pictured just inside the Washington, DC, border near New York Avenue, the Baltimore-Washington Parkway is being built overhead. Only 14 years later, the Pennsylvania Railroad would merge with the New York Central and close. (National Archives and Records Administration.)

Meanwhile, the era of the streetcar in Washington, DC, was closing as well. This image shows a DC Transit streetcar turning at Fourteenth Street and Colorado Avenue NW. In selling the system, the US Senate required the new owner to replace it with buses by 1963. The line paralleling US Route 1 closed in 1958. The last streetcar ran on January 1962. (National Capital Trolley Museum.)

Amtrak, or the National Railroad Passenger Corporation, was founded in 1971 to operate the few remaining passenger rail lines in the United States. After the failure of Penn Central, which was the result of the Baltimore & Ohio, Pennsylvania, and New York Central Railroads merging, Amtrak took ownership of the northeast corridor and began running trains between New York and Washington, DC, via the Baltimore-to-Washington route. (Amtrak.)

The Baltimore-Washington Parkway, conceived as an alternative to US Route 1, began construction in 1950 and was completed in 1954. The parkway was the first limited-access, divided highway in Maryland and was specifically routed to provide access to major federal government installations, such as Fort Meade and Greenbelt Park. Constructed under the Bureau of Public Roads and managed by the National Park Service, the parkway was designed to include a variable right-of-way with plantings and protected views. In the image above, road grading and landscaping are ongoing in 1951. The wide median and protected views are already evident. Below, the bridge crossing Riverdale Road is under construction, while Riverdale Road is routed around the bridge piers. This point is where East-West Highway meets Eastpines Shopping Center, which had not been built yet. (Both, National Archives and Records Administration.)

Construction of the Baltimore-Washington Parkway included designing for existing rail lines, roads, and rivers. The image above shows the rail line that extended from the Baltimore & Ohio toward Annapolis on the Washington, Baltimore & Annapolis Railway right-of-way. Wide, smooth highway construction has met the smaller country roads that wind toward the farm in the distance. In the image below, taken in 1957 after the road was completed, the parkway crosses the Patuxent River north of Laurel. Note the variable-width median with trees that were maintained during construction and the lack of billboards and advertising. Surprisingly, the view has not changed dramatically in the last 50 years. (Both, National Archives and Records Administration.)

In the image above, the US Park Police, which oversee the parkway as a National Park Service unit, are watching for speeders. The wide stretch of paved concrete was a dramatic difference from the US Route 1 experience. Faster cars meant that better policing was required. Meanwhile, the traffic on the parkway was, and still is, a major issue. At this exit in Cheverly, a long line of cars waits to exit onto Landover Road. While the orientation of the roads has not changed dramatically, the surrounding suburban landscape has added motels, offices, and commercial development. (Both, National Archives and Records Administration.)

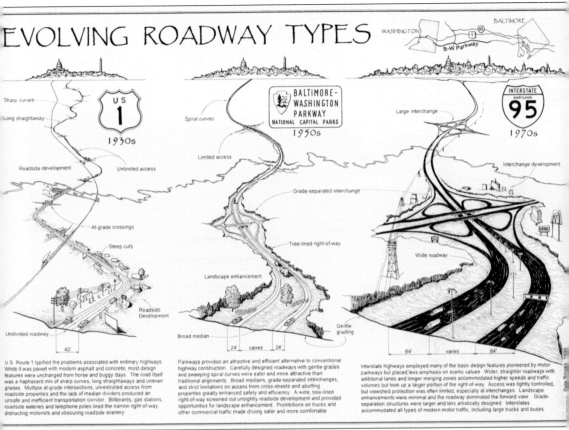

EVOLVING ROADWAY TYPES

WASHINGTON · B-W Parkway · BALTIMORE

US 1 · 1930s

Sharp curves · Long straightaway · Roadside development · Unlimited access · At-grade crossings · Steep cuts · Undivided roadway · Roadside Development · 40'

BALTIMORE-WASHINGTON PARKWAY · NATIONAL CAPITAL PARKS · 1950s

Spiral curves · Limited access · Grade-separated interchange · Tree-lined right-of-way · Landscape enhancement · Broad median · 24' varies 24'

INTERSTATE MARYLAND 95 · 1970s

Large interchange · Interchange development · Wide roadway · Gentle grading · 64' varies 64'

U.S. Route 1 typified the problems associated with ordinary highways. While it was paved with modern asphalt and concrete, most design features were unchanged from horse and buggy days. The road itself was a haphazard mix of sharp curves, long straightaways and uneven grades. Multiple at-grade intersections, unrestricted access from roadside properties and the lack of median dividers produced an unsafe and inefficient transportation corridor. Billboards, gas stations, roadside eateries and telephone poles lined the narrow right-of-way, distracting motorists and obscuring roadside scenery.

Parkways provided an attractive and efficient alternative to conventional highway construction. Carefully designed roadways with gentle grades and sweeping spiral curves were safer and more attractive than traditional alignments. Broad medians, grade-separated interchanges, and strict limitations on access from cross-streets and abutting properties greatly enhanced safety and efficiency. A wide, tree-lined right-of-way screened out unsightly roadside development and provided opportunities for landscape enhancement. Prohibitions on trucks and other commercial traffic made driving safer and more comfortable.

Interstate highways employed many of the basic design features pioneered by motor parkways but placed less emphasis on scenic values. Wider, straighter roadways with additional lanes and longer merging zones accommodated higher speeds and traffic volumes but took up a larger portion of the right-of-way. Access was tightly controlled, but viewshed protection was often limited, especially at interchanges. Landscape enhancements were minimal and the roadway dominated the forward view. Grade-separation structures were larger and less artistically designed. Interstates accommodated all types of modern motor traffic, including large trucks and buses.

The Historic American Building Survey created a comparison of road types that were common in the Baltimore-to-Washington corridor as part of the documentation of the Baltimore-Washington Parkway. This comparison is important to see how the roads changed over time. US Route 1, with at-grade crossings, roadside development, and unlimited access, represented a slow-movement type of road that had become too choked with traffic and development to be used safely. The goal of the parkway was to create grade separations, gentle elevation changes, and a landscaped, tree-lined right-of-way. This encouraged faster movement while creating a pleasant experience. Finally, the new interstates that arrived just a few years later were designed for even faster speeds, wider roads, and very limited access. While the US Route 1 model was bad for traffic and speed, the parkway and interstate models were bad for communities, which had been bypassed and left behind in favor of standardized, sterilized interchange-based development. (Library of Congress.)

113

Interstate 895, originally the Harbor Tunnel Thruway, crossed the Patapsco River south of Baltimore to avoid downtown streets. The tunnel and approaches opened in 1957. The image above shows the US Route 1 approach to the interchange at Elkridge in 1959. The Maxwell Diner still exists, but note the reduced traffic, now shifted to major highways. This new Thruway would connect with highways north of Baltimore, eliminating over 50 stop lights. The Baltimore Beltway opened in stages between 1955 and 1962, forming the first beltway in the United States. The image below from 1959 shows the Alternate US Route 1 interchange, known as Washington Boulevard where the old US Route 1 alignment changed to Southwestern Boulevard at Halethorpe. The wide-open interstate style stands in stark comparison to the parkway model. (Both, National Archives and Records Administration.)

The Washington, DC–area Capital Beltway was conceived in the 1940s, and design work began in the early 1950s. The original plan called for work to begin near Beltsville and continue counterclockwise around the Washington area and across the Potomac to connect with US Route 1 in Virginia, thus bypassing US Route 1 through the most congested parts of the road in the region. However, the plan was amended to add an eastern portion over the Potomac River and back to the Baltimore-Washington Parkway at Greenbelt. The first section of the highway was opened in 1961, and the entire beltway was finished in 1964. While the plan was to reduce traffic, explosive development around the Beltway has created some of the slowest traffic in the United States. (Both, National Archives and Records Administration.)

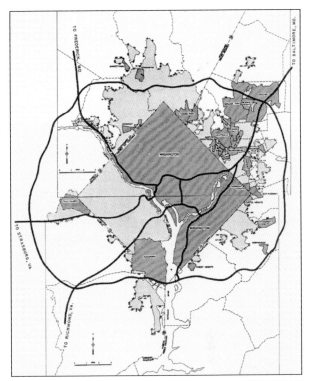

This photograph shows Interstate 95 under construction at Gunpowder Road in Beltsville. The main grade of the interstate is below the bridge under construction. Interstate 95, which connected the East Coast, was originally intended to cut directly through the middle of Washington, DC, via a route that would have roughly followed the Green and Red Lines on the Metro. (DC Public Library, Washington Star Collection.)

Steaming past the Thomas Viaduct, a last hurrah of a steam engine parallels the brand-new Harbor Tunnel Thruway. This photograph of old and new was taken from Lawyer's Hill, where Union soldiers stood sentry during the Civil War. The Thomas Viaduct is often overlooked by those speeding by on Interstate 895, and the view from this point on Lawyer's Hill is hard to come by today. (Elkridge Heritage Society.)

The 1970s continued a long period of disinvestment in the US Route 1 corridor. The photograph at right represents a time in Hyattsville when automobiles were the primary users of the highway. Lustine Auto Sales dominated the region, with new and used cars, repair shops, and services. Residential and commercial buildings have been leveled and removed, replaced by a variety of condominiums and restaurants today. Below, looking south on US Route 1 in Elkridge, traffic has dwindled significantly with the new highways. On the far left is Layton's service station. This era of highways is, unfortunately, what many remember about US Route 1. (Right, DC Public Library, Special Collections; below, Elkridge Heritage Society.)

College Park's motel collection was waning by the 1970s. Howard Johnson's would become Plato's Diner, which closed in 2016 after a fire. US Route 1 continues up the hill toward University Park. Park University Hotel, with its sharply pointed entry, has been replaced by a simplified entry to the Quality Inn. Both were purchased by the University of Maryland in 2016. (Prince George's County Historical Society.)

The Colony 7 Motel was built just to the east of US Route 1, surrounded by Fort Meade. With 200 rooms and Schrafft's Restaurant and Cocktail Lounge, the Colony 7 was a premier hotel in the region. Every weekend, there was a dinner theater show. Today, the main building is used for the National Cryptologic Museum and is located on Colony 7 Road. (Meredith Gorres.)

The history of flight in the region took another major step with NASA Goddard Space Flight Center (SFC) opening in 1959. Using land carved out of the larger Beltsville Agricultural Research Center, the center was intended to be the main control site for launches in the United States. Goddard SFC managed Project Mercury until the scope outstripped the space available at the site. The role of managing manned flight was passed to Johnson Space Center in Houston, Texas. Goddard SFC's role was then transitioned to space and earth science. The site is responsible for the development of space communications, long range telescopes such as Hubble, and satellites that study Earth's climate. The image above shows the opening of the facility in 1959, while at right is the first American meteorological satellite, TIROS. (Both, National Aeronautics and Space Administration.)

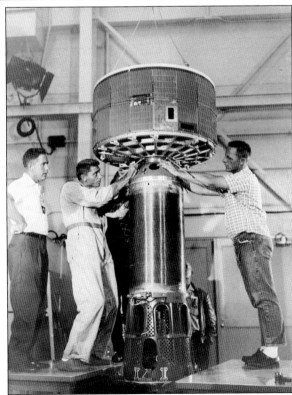

One of the last major transportation innovations that occurred in the region before the 1990s was the Metro system, operated by Washington Metropolitan Transit Agency (WMATA). While calls for a subway system had started as early as the 1950s, during the last days of the streetcar, WMATA was not started until 1967. Ground was broken in 1969, and the first stages opened in 1976. The image below shows workers, sometimes known as sandhogs, digging the tunnels for the system. The New Carrollton Station, above, was built along the old Pennsylvania Railroad line, shown here with two GG-1 engines used by Amtrak. The station was built to serve Metro, commuter rail, and long-distance rail and was finished in 1978. (Above, Prince George's County Historical Society; below, DC Public Library.)

Six

THE ROUTE 1 CORRIDOR TODAY

1990–PRESENT

US Route 1 has changed dramatically over the last 300 years. From a simple road through the woods to a dirt road with the first airplanes flying above to a traffic-clogged highway bypassed by major interstates, the region has seen major changes in transportation history. The Lustine Center in Hyattsville is a legacy of that change—from automobile showroom to fitness center. (Author's collection.)

Lake Artemisia is another example of changing transportation. The lake was enlarged from smaller goldfish ponds within the majority–African American Lakeland neighborhood by WMATA, which removed parts of the neighborhood and used the soil for the Metro Green Line. Today, the lake is a community asset for College Park and Berwyn Heights with walking and biking trails. (Maryland–National Capital Park and Planning Commission.)

Trails represent the next major transportation change. Harkening to the Good Roads Movement, these trails represent an environmentally friendly option to beat traffic and avoid stress. Trails now connect the region in and around US Route 1, south of the Capital Beltway, to downtown Washington, DC. The lines of both the Washington, Baltimore & Annapolis, and the Capital Transit trolley have also been converted to trails. (State of Maryland.)

A MARC train arrives at College Park. MARC, or Maryland Area Regional Commuter train, is administered by the Maryland Transit Authority. Operating on three lines, the MARC system uses the Camden and Penn Lines through the Baltimore-to-Washington region. Stops are available at St. Denis, Dorsey, Jessup, Savage, Laurel, Beltsville, Greenbelt, College Park, Riverdale Park, and Washington's Union Station, paralleling the old Baltimore & Ohio Railroad. (Author's collection.)

The historic legacy of aviation in the region has been documented at the College Park Aviation Museum. Opened in 1998, the museum has a library, auditorium, and displays of the 1910 Wright Model B, 1911 Curtiss Model 9, Berliner Helicopter, and ERCO Ercoupe. The airfield is still an active landing strip, though access within the Washington, DC, flight zone is restricted to authorized planes. (Anacostia Trails Heritage Area Inc.)

College Park demonstrates new changes to the US Route 1 region. A new hotel opened in 2017 across from the University of Maryland's main entrance. Combined with new restaurants, condominium construction in Hyattsville, new development in Mount Rainier, and the potential for new federal installations in Greenbelt, the southern part of US Route 1 has seen major growth in the first years of the 21st century. (City of College Park.)

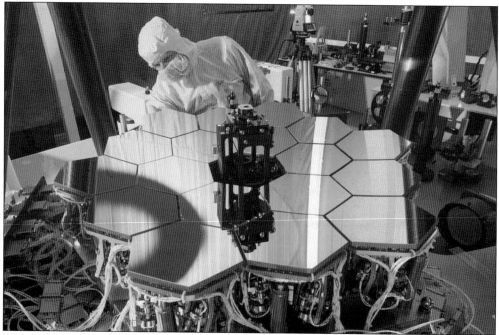

The James Webb Telescope is the newest space-observing satellite telescope to be overseen by the scientists at NASA Goddard SFC. Developed in cooperation with the European and Canadian space agencies, the telescope is scheduled to launch in October 2018. Once in orbit, it will unfold to create a 6.5-meter gold reflector. The history of flight will continue well into the future. (NASA.)

US Route 1's legacy as a connection to communities and a corridor of innovation continues into today. While the road has changed significantly over time, from horse-drawn carts to half-ton pick-up trucks, the history made along the road continues. Communications history related to post roads, the telegraph, airmail, and satellites has been made here. Transportation developments from rolling roads, the Baltimore & Ohio Railroad, streetcars, the Baltimore-Washington Parkway, the Capital Beltway, the Harbor Tunnel Thruway, Amtrak, and Metro have been made here. Aviation history, from the earliest balloons to steps on the moon, is well represented in one corridor. But many places that are remembered by those who have traveled this road—One Spot Flea Remover, Little Tavern, diners, motels, and gas stations—have disappeared. For this reason, this publication documents and celebrates the legacy of US Route 1 and the surrounding corridor. (Author's collection.)

BIBLIOGRAPHY

Belasco, Warren James. *Americans on the Road: From Autocamp to Motel 1910–1945*. Cambridge, MA: MIT Press, 1981.

Genovese, Peter. *The Great American Road Trip: US 1 Maine to Florida*. New Brunswick, NJ: Rutgers University Press, 1999.

Jackson, J.B. "Other Directed Houses." *Landscape in Sight: Looking at America*. Helen Lefkowitz Horowitz, ed. New Haven, CT: Yale University Press, 1997.

Jackson, Kenneth. *Crabgrass Frontier: The Suburbanization of the United States*. New York, NY: Oxford University Press, 1985.

Jakle, John, and Keith Sculle. *Fast Food: Roadside Restaurants in the Automobile Age*. Baltimore, MD: Johns Hopkins Press, 1999.

———. *Remembering Roadside America: Preserving the Recent Past as Landscape and Place*. Knoxville, TN: University of Tennessee Press, 2011.

———. *The Gas Station in America*. Baltimore, MD: Johns Hopkins Press, 1994.

Jakle, John, Keith Sculle, and Jefferson Rogers. *The Motel in America*. Baltimore, MD: Johns Hopkins Press, 1996.

Langdon, Philip. *Orange Roofs, Golden Arches: The Architecture of American Chain Restaurants*. New York, NY: Alfred A. Knopf, 1986.

Liebs, Chester. *From Main Street to Miracle Mile: American Roadside Architecture*. Baltimore, MD: Johns Hopkins Press, 1995.

Marriott, Paul Daniel. *Saving Historic Roads*. New York, NY: John Wiley & Sons, 1998.

Tomlan, Michael, ed. *Preservation of What, for Whom: A Critical Look at Historical Significance*. Ithaca, NY: National Council for Preservation Education, 1998.

Vieyra, David. *Fill 'Er Up: An Architectural History of America's Gasoline Stations*. New York, NY: Macmillan, 1979.

Virta, Alan. *Prince George's County: A Pictorial History*. Brookfield, MO: The Donning Company, 1991.

About the Maryland Heritage Areas Program

This publication supports the interpretive efforts of two of the Maryland Heritage Areas Program management entities. The Maryland Heritage Areas Authority provides targeted financial and technical assistance within 13 locally designated Heritage Areas, each of which has a distinct focus or theme that represents a unique aspect of Maryland's character. Anacostia Trails Heritage Area Inc. and the associated brand mark "Maryland Milestones," is the management organization for the northern Prince George's County region around US Route 1 from Mount Rainier to Laurel, while Patapsco Heritage Greenway Inc. serves as the management entity for a region around Howard and Baltimore County near Elkridge. Together, the Maryland Heritage Areas Authority, the Heritage Areas, and local partners support the economic well-being of Maryland's communities by promoting, sustaining, and creating place-based experiences for visitors and residents alike.

www.marylandmilestones.org

www.patapsco.org

mht.maryland.gov

Discover Thousands of Local History Books Featuring Millions of Vintage Images

Arcadia Publishing, the leading local history publisher in the United States, is committed to making history accessible and meaningful through publishing books that celebrate and preserve the heritage of America's people and places.

Find more books like this at
www.arcadiapublishing.com

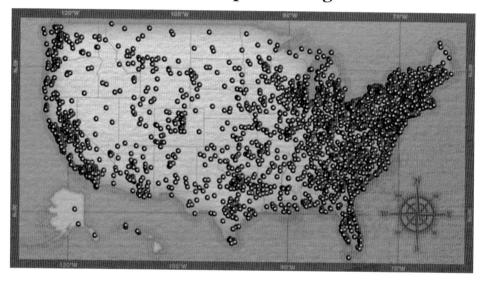

Search for your hometown history, your old stomping grounds, and even your favorite sports team.